Re-Emerging Russia and India Russia Relations

Re-Emerging Russia and India Russia Relations

Prof. R.G. Gidadhubli

KALPAZ

First Published, 2020
Published by

Kalpaz Publications
C-30, Satyawati Nagar,
Delhi – 110052
Ph.: 011-47034999, 9811692060
www.kalpazpublications.com
E-mail: kalpaz@hotmail.com

Printed at: Gyan Press, Delhi

Cataloging in Publication Data—DK
Courtesy: D.K. Agencies (P) Ltd. <docinfo@dkagencies.com>

Gidadhubli, R. G., author.
Re-emerging Russia and India Russia relations / Prof. R.G. Gidadhubli.
pages cm
ISBN 9789353242824

1. Russia (Federation)—Foreign relations. 2. Economic development—Russia (Federation) 3. Russia (Federation)—Politics and government. 4. Russia (Federation)—Foreign relations—India. 5. India—Foreign relations—Russia (Federation) I. Title.

LCC DK66.G53 2020 | DDC 327.47 23

Contents

Section III - India-Russia Economic Relations

Preface

In the first section there are six papers. The First paper published in World Focus Journal in 2011 is entitled "Russia's Two Decades of Turbulent Phases of Economic Transition from Communism to Capitalism". The focus is to highlight political and economic objectives of Russia to bring about transition from the former Soviet era totalitarian Communist system to market oriented Capitalist economic system during the first two decades after the Soviet breakup in 1991. Developments under different phases are discussed - (a) from Communism to Wild Capitalism: (b) from Wild Capitalism to State Capitalism and (c) from State Capitalism to Market Capitalism.

Policy decisions taken by the Russian successive presidents, namely Boris Yeltsin, Dmitri Medvedev and Vladimir Putin are discussed as also shortcomings, failures and achievements. For instance, issues relating to Shock Therapy, privatisation, price liberalisation, unemployment as also reversal to policy decisions are discussed. It is contended that the path of transition was not smooth but has been painful for a large section of society.

The Second paper entitled "Boris Yeltsin's Controversial Legacy" published in *Economic and Political Weekly* (EPW) highlights varied and contradictory assessments of his leadership of Russia. The Western leaders appreciated his role in the breakup of the former Soviet Union in 1991 and his pro-West policies changing World History and undertaking policy decisions to bring about democracy in One Stroke. At the same time there are many analysts who criticised him for his policy of Shock Therapy that brought a class of Oligarchs and New Russians in Russia and disaster and economic crisis for Russians leading to hyper inflation, economic disparities and unemployment for millions of people in the country.

The Third paper "Refurbishing the Military Industrial Complex" published in *EPW* deals with the problems and disasters caused by the neglect of defence sector in the aftermath the breakup of the USSR and efforts being made by Vladimir Putin after taking over presidency of Russia to upgrade and modernise defence sector in order to make Russia re-emerge as a major exporter of arms in the world.

The Fourth paper "Is Russia's Crackdown on NGO's Justifiable?" published in *Mainstream* deals with differences among political parties in Russia on law passed by the Russian government on 'Random Checking of NGOs' in 2013 contending that NGOs being funded from abroad operated as instruments of the West to influence Russian society. NGO has been a relatively new phenomenon in post-Soviet Russia and there were accusations that many NGO's were involved in political activities as foreign agents creating instability in the country.

The Fifth paper "Two Decades of Putin's Leadership of Russia" published in *NAM Journal* in January 2020 highlights his achievements and challenges. Effort has been made as to analyse how Putin was able to handle with iron hand several problems facing Russia on domestic political front and external relations. Mention may be made of conflict with Georgia, annexation of Crimea in 2014, controlling Communist Party and centralisation of power in Kremlin. With rising oil prices since 2008, Russia emerged as a major exporter of oil to become 'Energy Super Power' with huge inflow of petrodollars and that enhanced Putin's popularity who also focused on defence. At the same time Russia faced demographic decline and economic sanctions imposed by the West. Putin who was against the Soviet disintegration has his vision of creating 'Reunion' of three states namely, Russia, Belo-Russia and Ukraine which may remain his dream.

The Sixth paper "Putin's Bombshehll: Real Change for Russia"? published in Mainstream in February 2020 focuses on Putin's address to the Russian Parliament Duma to bring about major changes in the political structure through Constitutional reforms giving more authority to Parliament transferring from the President. On this issue Kremlin critic Alexei Navalny has contended that by declaring for 'Change', Putin intends to retain power after his term ends in 2024.

The second section comprise of eight papers.

The Seventh paper "Russia-China Relations-Role of Far East" published in Mainstream in Sept-Oct 2005 highlights efforts made by the Russian President Putin during his summit meeting with the Chinese president in Moscow in July 2005 to strengthen bilateral strategic cooperation by resolving long standing historic border dispute, enhancing trade and economic ties and containing threat perception of Chinese expansion and 'Yellow Danger' by millions of Chinese citizens living in Russia's Far East. It is contended that Putin has created a new era in Russia-China relations to overcome conflicts with the West and strengthen Russia's position in the world.

The Eight paper "Re-emergence of Russia: Implications for Southeast Asia" was presented at the 22nd Asia Pacific Roundtable in Kuala Lumpur in June 2008. It is argued that Russia intended to pursue 'Look East' policy as a part of strengthening its global importance by Putin's visit to several Southeast countries. In the paper several issues are highlighted concerning Russia's growing conflict with the West, increasing political and economic relations with Southeast Asian countries, as also nuclear energy cooperation, defence production cooperation and exports to Malaysia, Vietnam, Indonesia and Thailand.

The Ninth paper "Contribution of India and Russia in the Evolving International Order" was presented at the Workshop in Mumbai University. International order was undergoing major changes from bipolar world to multi-polar world, emergence of several regional organisations such as RIC, BRICS and SCO in which India and Russia were actively participating. It is pointed out that tenth Trilateral meeting of India, Russia and China held in Wuhan in China in November 2010 focused on plans for coordination of actions in Asia-Pacific Region in dealing with economic, political and security related issues. The leaders of Russia and USA strengthened bilateral ties at their summit meetings at G-20, APEC and NATO in November 2010 signing of new START Treaty in April 2010 and US support to Russia for accession to WTO in October 2010. With the end of cold war era, economic liberalisation was taking place bringing about paradigm shift in evolving international order in which India and Russia independently and jointly played significant role.

The Tenth paper "Embargo Versus Sanctions: Tit for Tat between Russia and West" A New Cold War? is published in *Mainstream* in September 2015. Due to Russia's annexation of Crimea in 2014, the USA and West European countries which alleged it was illegal claiming it was part of Ukraine, wanted to punish Russia by imposing economic sanctions to hurt Russian economic development. In retaliation, in August 2015 the Russian government declared policy of embargo on imports of consumer goods from the West. In the process of Tit for Tat thousands of tons of goods including food products of West were destroyed by Russia that were badly needed for millions of common people. The Russian government undertook policy of import restrictions for promoting domestic production and favouring imports from BRICS countries and India. Impact of consequences and counter-arguments of political strategy are discussed.

The Eleventh paper is entitled "Cost and Benefit of Russia's Entry into WTO" published in *Mainstream* in October 2012. Russia was admitted to WTO as 156th member in August 2012 which added another feather to Putin's cap subsequent to Russia becoming member of several international organisations such as G-8, G-20 and APEC. But there were critics in Russia including few Communist leaders who argued that WTO was 'Economic NATO', Russia was entering WTO at a wrong time due to global recession, Russia will face economic decline since it cannot compete with the West, unemployment will increase etc. But disagreeing with criticism, it was contended that Russia waited for 20 years to get membership since long time was required to comply with conditionalities, costs will be compensated by benefits Russia getting advanced technology from West, Russia cannot remain isolated in era of economic globalisation and so on. However, challenges persist.

The Twelfth paper "Complexities of Russia-NATO Relations: Growing Conflicts" has been published in World Focus in June 2016. In contrast to decades of enemical ties between the former Soviet Union and NATO, initiatives taken by post-Soviet Russia in the 1990's undertaking pro-West policies and in dissolving Warsaw Pact, evolving 'Constructive Cooperation' etc. promoted cooperation between Russia and NATO. But much against Russia's hope and expectations, NATO was not dissolved and in fact expanded towards the East involving not only few East European countries but also Baltic States of the former Soviet Union. Moreover, NATO's decision of installation of military bases in the Baltic region caused concern for Russia as a security threat resulting in growing mutual conflicts during the last decade. The Russian President Vladimir Putin approved New Military Policy in 2014 to counter policy measures of NATO.

The Thirteenth paper "Trump-Putin Helsinki Summit: Advantage Russia" published in *Mainstream* in August 2018 highlights the significance of bilateral relations between Russia and USA. From the American perspective the outcome of the Summit was far from satisfactory but the Russian Foreign Minister Sergei Lavrov maintained that many global issues were discussed and it was the 'first step' in improving bilateral relations. There are many critics who accuse Russia in meddling in the US election getting Trump elected as president and hence who is soft towards Russia.

The Fourteenth paper "Russia's 'Vostok 2018' Military Exercises-Putin's Show of Strength?" was published in *Mainstream* in September 2018. Kremlin spokesman Dmitry Peskov was candid in stating that Russia conducted this large scale military exercise to showcase its defence capability in international situation which was unfriendly towards Russia. Perhaps he has in mind the timing when Russia was supporting the Syrian president al-Asad while USA was supporting his opposition leaders in war in Syria and NATO was conducting flurry of military drills near Russia's borders. Vladimir Putin has increased the budget for defence sector in order to upgrade and modernise military capability.

The Third Section comprises of four papers.

The Fifteenth paper "India's Exports to Russia-Complexities and Contradictions" was published in *EPW* in November 1995. Economic liberalisation was taking place in both the countries and Russia was undergoing major transition from communist system to market economy. So far as India's exports to Russia was concerned, there were growing complexities in bilateral ties from discontinuity of Rupee Trade system that was evolved by India and the former USSR and prevailed for decades, there were multiplicities of trade channels, lack of transparency for release of debt repayment funds, uncertainties and irrationalities in Russia's import regulations and tax structure, underdeveloped banking system in Russia, from legal trade to illegal trade, role of some emerging unscrupulous elements and fly-by-night operators of India to make quick money and so on.

The Sixteenth research paper "India-Russia Economic Relations: Challenges and Opportunities" submitted at the University workshop for discussion. It was written after the visit of Vladimir Putin to India in October 2000 when he met not only the Indian Prime Minister and high level state officials but also 350 CEO's of India's leading industrial firms in Mumbai that was organised by the CM. The paper makes in depth analysis of strengthening bilateral relations as both the countries signed a Declaration of Strategic Partnership. Issues concerning defence imports by India and importance of nine agreements signed covering fields of science and technology, banking, agriculture, exploration of natural gas are highlighted. Effort has been made to analyze issues concerning economic development of Russia on trade with India and role of leading Indian groups such as CII, FICCI for promoting trade and joint ventures. Problems facing Russian economy have been discussed as also Putin's economic priorities and need to evolve appropriate trade strategies for India.

The Seventeenth paper "India-Russia Economic Ties: trends, constraints and prospects" published in World Focus in August 2008 highlights the fact that trade and economic ties had badly suffered after the Soviet breakup during the period 1991 to 2007 even as political relations were close and consistent. While India's exports significantly declined, imports from Russia were increasing. India's traditional items of export such as tea, coffee, textiles in which India had monopoly position were affected. It is stated that main causes for decline were chaotic political and economic conditions in Russia, breakdown of old institutions, role of mafia, complexities of debt repayment system, high risk factors, 'information gap' about Russia's new institutions etc. Basic data of imports and exports has been provided. It is stated that initiatives were taken by both the governments and trading associations to promote trade. On that basis possible alternative scenarios for trade turnover -optimistic, pessimistic and pragmatic for medium term are highlighted.

The Eighteenth paper "India-Russia Bilateral Relations are Intensifying but Challenges Persist" was published in *World Focus* in November 2016. It is stated that the Indian Prime Minister Mr Narendra Modi had met the Russian President Mr Vladimir Putin several times at G-20, SCO and BRICS meetings reconfirming the chemistry of close and cordial bilateral relations. In the paper efforts made by both the countries to intensify bilateral ties in several fields, namely nuclear technology programmes, defence sector, energy sector, economic ties are highlighted and analyzed. Russia has played a pioneering role in setting up 25 nuclear power plants in India enhancing India's status globally when the Western powers denied assistance in this field. In the defence sector India and Russia share a 'special and privileged strategic relationship' by providing hi-tech defence equipments including missiles, multifunctional fighters, Sukhoi Superjets and supporting India to become 35th member of Missile Technology Control Regime and Nuclear Supplier Group.

It is pointed out that Russia has been a major exporter of oil and natural gas to India and supported participation of India's ONGC in joint offshore projects.

Trade and economic ties continue to be weak despite 'Druzba-Dosti' vision of Vladimir Putin and hence an effort has been made to analyze problems and challenges facing both the countries even as both the countries have ambitious plan to achieve target of $ 30 billion trade turnover by 2025 from the prevailing level of about $ 15 billion. Constraints and challenges facing business communities of both the countries such as long time and high cost of transportation to export to Russia, high tax rates, negative information about marketing conditions, information gap, bureaucratic hurdles and restrictive policies and so on.

Acknowledgement

The book mainly contains articles and papers published in eminent journals, and hence I express my deep sense of gratitude to the Chief Editors and Editorial Committee members of well-known journals – 'Economic and Political Weekly', 'Mainstream', 'World Focus' and 'NAM Today'. I thank Russian and western media and reports of analysts which has helped me for information and analysis on Russia for my write-ups. I wish to convey my gratitude to UGC and Mumbai University authorities who gave me opportunity, having studied in Moscow, to promote Soviet studies and serve the University for over four decades and fulfill my objective of carrying out teaching and research on the former Soviet Union and post-Soviet Republics including Russia and Central Asia and relations with India. I express my appreciation to my former colleagues and staff in the Center and thanks to my close friend Prof P.M. Kamath for recommending me to approach Gyan Books for my publication. I express my sincere gratitude to Mr Amit Garg, Chief of Gyan Books and all staff members of Gyan Books for publishing my book.

Section I - Russia Macro Analysis: Political and Economic Developments

1

Russia's Two Decades of Turbulent Phases of Economic Transition: from Communism to Capitalism

During the last two decades Russia has passed through several phases in its economic objective of bringing about transition from its former totalitarian communist system to market oriented capitalist economic system. The country has been led during this period by three presidents— two terms of Boris Yeltsin, two terms of Vladimir Putin and one term of Dmitri Medvedev. An effort has been made in this paper to analyze policy measures undertaken from time to time as also the performance and problems faced by the country under different phases of economic development.

Phase I — From Communism to Wild Capitalism—Decade of Crisis

In the aftermath of Soviet breakup, Russia inherited economic system which was based on communist ideology comprising state ownership of means of production and centralised planning of all economic activities. In this background, the main objective of independent Russia was to bring about transition to political democracy and market economy which was difficult and painful. It also meant reversal from communism to capitalism, which meant negation of the Marxian Ideological concept that communism is the ultimate socio-economic formation of the society. In the post-Soviet era, even as each former communist country adopted its own path of transition, Russia under the leadership of Boris Yeltsin chose Shock Therapy (ST) rather than Gradualist Approach. Apart from the advice of western experts including Andrei Aslund and former IMF Chief Michael Camdesus, Yeltsin and his close associates had their own interest in ST model which meant economic transition in one-stroke. Yeltsin's had two-fold objectives for his choice of ST based on his own policy political perspective under uncertain and chaotic politic-economic condition. Firstly, to prevent the return of frustrated thousands of Soviet era communists regaining power and secondly, to make the choice of free market economy irreversible. What encouraged Yeltsin was that Russia also received external financial assistance for adopting radical reform measures.

Be that as it may, the basic elements of ST were liberalisation of prices, privatisation of state property, elimination of state monopoly on trade and macro-economic stabilisation. Being over-enthusiastic and confident of his policy decisions, Yeltsin liberalised prices in one stroke in 1992 for a large number of goods. He also pushed through the policy of mass privatisation also known as Voucher Privatisation under which each citizen of Russia was given voucher of 1,000 Rubles to buy shares in about 14,000 privatised enterprises. He claimed that he made 144 million Russians feel rich overnight. Further Russia also implemented Cash Privatisation policy by selling state-held shares for money to mobilize resources, which was much needed for the government. Thus, by the end of 1993 over 83 thousand, that is about one-third enterprises were privatised.

Western analysts complimented Yeltsin for policy implementation and taking Russia on the course of market economy. But the impact of Yeltsin's policies on the economy and on the large section of population was disastrous and unprecedented. Russia was plunged into deep economic crisis which was reflected in sharp decline in Gross Domestic Product and hyper inflation which is evident from the following data published by Economic Intelligence Reports

Year	*1992*	*1994*	*1996*	*1998*	*2000*
Annual GDP	-14.5	-12.7	-3.5	-4.6	6.3
Inflation	1354	307	48	28	21

The period of 1992-96 was the worst when average annual GDP declined by over 10 percent per annum and country experienced hyper inflation. As compared to the first half of the decade, the rate of economic fall somewhat declined in the second half of the 1990's. By the end of the decade there was positive though modest growth rates in the economy. The magnitude of economic decline was so severe that the industrial output was almost half of what it was in 1991 which meant virtual deindustrialisation of the economy. The real sectors of the economy and the technological levels of enterprises suffered very badly. The Federal budget as percentage of GDP continued to be negative till 1999. Similarly, Russia's external debt which was negligible at $ 79 bn in 1992 went up to $160 bn in 1999. At the same time Russia failed to bring about much needed reforms in banking and financial sectors as a result of which there was mushroom growth of banks which cheated millions of innocent people promising fast growth of their hard earned money. *Ruble* was devalued in 1998 which had already lost its value on which it was printed. Hence thousands of Russians living in large cities with whatever left of their hard earned life savings preferred to hold their money in dollars rather than in Rubles. Under conditions of absence of stable monetary system and Ruble losing its value, barter system and shadow economy prevailed in the country.

Since normal economic activities were badly affected, workers in factories and shops were retrenched on a large scale. While the former USSR claimed full employment, Russia faced major problem of unemployment reaching the level of about 20 million in 1999. In many regions workers were retrenched and those kept on jobs were often paid partly in kind of whatever they were producing since managers lacked resources and were not able to run factories due to sharp decline in demand for their goods. Over and above prevailing hyper inflation led to impoverishment of a large section of society. As a result of which Russia faced very serious social consequences including rise in crimes and beggary. Moreover, with deteriorating health care system, death rate increased and birthrate declined and average life expectancy declined from 73 years in 1990 to about 57 years in 2001. Total population in the country declined by about 10 million in a decade and total population of Russia was 143 million in 2002. This demographic decline has caused serious social and economic consequences for Russia.

At the same time ironically Russia experienced another extremity in society that is the emerging new super-rich class known as New Russians some of whom became millionaires and multi-millionaires in a short span of a decade. They were connected with energy or banking sectors and were either well connected politically or were former party *apparatchiks*. This was possible due to Yeltsin's blunder of hasty implementation of the policy of privatisation when the valuation system of state property was not evolved. Hence as rightly observed by Anatoly Zhelenyak 'property yielded power and power yielded property' Yeltsin's privatisation was virtually Grabification of state property by few at the cost of the larger interest of the country. In essence policies of privatisation, liberalisation were misused by vested groups leading to rise of oligarchs who started controlling economy leading to what some critics call 'Wild Capitalism' or 'Robber Baron' capitalism in Russia. In the ultimate analysis while the Soviet era Communist system was officially dissolved, much expected normal and true market economic system did not emerge. A large section of population of Russia continue to pay a heavy price for economic blunders committed by Yeltsin.

Phase II — From Wild Capitalism to State Capitalism—Period of Recovery and Boom

Vladimir Putin who succeeded Yeltsin was one of his close associates and was already prime minister of Russia. Putin's two terms of presidency covering 1999-2008 was an important phase in Russia's contemporary economic history. During the first four-year term, there was modest economic growth with Gross Domestic Product (GDP) rate of about four percent per annum. This was a positive change and economy started recovering from the negative and dismal performance prevailing during previous decade. The second term of presidency was marked by dramatic shift in growth performance when Russian economy experienced boom with fairly high GDP annual growth rates of six to eight percent. What is equally important was that while there was no major change during the first term, Putin brought about major shift in policies. In fact, there was reversal of policy measures which were initiated by Boris Yeltsin, particularly with regard to economic liberalisation and privatisation. Putin and his policy advisors close to Kremlin at that time possibly had two-fold objectives. Firstly, to rectify fallout of irrational and ST policies committed during the period of crisis particularly hasty privatisation. Secondly, being a former official in KGB, Putin decided to reassert strong state control over commanding heights of economy particularly on energy and defence sectors and also on regions.

It needs to be mentioned that a major factor which contributed to economic boom was the prevailing high international prices for hydrocarbon resources. Russia has all along been a major producer and exporter of oil and natural gas in the world. Hence when international oil prices were rising during the period 2003-2008, Russia's state treasury was getting filled with petrodollars and gold and hard currency reserves, which reached its peak of about $ 597 billion when oil prices touched $ 149 per barrel in the middle of 2008. Ruble appreciated against dollar from about 32 to 28 Rubles per dollar. Russia enjoyed surplus budget and foreign trade performance was impressive with surplus on trade account. Hence Putin could legitimately claim credit for bringing down external debt of the country from $ 130 bn in 1999 to $ 41 bn in July 2008.

Not only was the state treasury filled with gold and hard currency reserves exceeding $ 500 bn, but GDP per capita also rose to $ 9,075 in 2008. The average income of a large section of Russian population increased giving a big push for public consumption in the country, which also gave a boost to Putin's popularity rate as the best leader of Russia. Objectively speaking in effect Russian economy experienced consumption led growth rather than investment led growth. Because this rising consumer demand was met by imports because on the domestic front, there was persistent decrease in the production as also quality and competitiveness of Russian goods as compared to imported goods. In fact, this was not in the national long term interest as opined by analysts and hence should have been a matter of great concern to the policy-makers and corrective steps should have been taken urgently.

Hence in essence overdependence on oil exports has been a major negative factor for economic growth during Putin's presidency. On this issue there are strong arguments by some Russian analysts that due to this over dependence on oil exports there was no urge to undertake reform measures for the diversification and modernisation of the economy. In fact, some policy measures were initiated for reforming the economy during the first term of presidency of Putin. But by 2003 when oil prices started rising, there was complacency among the leading policy-makers and reform process slowed down.

Putin's policy shortcomings

Economic phase during Putin's presidency was marked by several shortcomings. Firstly, Russia did not rationally utilise huge inflow of petrodollars for economic modernisation and development of the country. On the other hand, huge amount of hard currency resources were used for acquisition of energy assets from foreign companies operating in Russia such as TNK-BP and thereby reducing the share of foreign firms and increasing the share of the Russian state and Russian energy companies. This was done as a part of the state policy of promoting 'Resource Nationalism'. But this has negative effect on foreign firms investing and operating in Russia.

Secondly, Russia's partly state-owned energy giants such as Gazprom, Rosneft Lukoil with due state support also acquired energy assets in other oil rich foreign countries including Central Asia, Algeria. Libya, Venezuela, etc. using the huge petrodollar funds accumulated due to high oil prices. It was evident that the underlying geo-political objective had been to make Russia Energy Super Power.

Thirdly, while thanks to inflow of petrodollars, Russia managed to repay substantial part of the country's debt to international institutions including World Bank, Paris Club etc. and thus reduced state debt it is reported that the hard currency reserves were also partly utilised for debt repayment of some Russian millionaire oligarchs.

Systemic Causes

Apart from the oil factor there were other serious systemic causes which have contributed to Russia's economic problems. There were also subjective factors including policy failures during Putin's presidency. Firstly, despite having necessary financial resources, adequate funds were not directed for diversifying the economy. In fact, diversification of the economy was not a priority of the policy-makers. For instance, resources were not invested for the development and modernisation of engineering and hi-tech branches of industry. Similarly, much needed infrastructure development was not given due attention when country had enough resources. Thus, Russia has lost an opportunity in modernising the economy and making it efficient and competitive.

Secondly, under Putin's presidency the level of centralisation in management and decision making had increased. Russia has 89 regions which were regrouped into seven macro regions by Putin and they were brought under direct control of the president. As opined by some western analysts Siloviki (pushers) comprising personnel of intelligence units and bureaucrats, who had close links with the Kremlin exercised major role in decision-making in political and economic issues of Russia. While this regrouping was possibly intended for political stability and control, according to some analysts that affected economic development indirectly since regions did not have much say in the economic development and problems of their regions. Subsequently, this became an important issue. For instance, as reported by the Russia's News Agency Interrfax in June 2009, the regional chief of Bashkortostan Murtaza Rakhimov created a minor scandal by comparing the level of centralisation in Russia to that of the Soviet era. The heads of regions put the onus on economic problems on the central leadership.

Thirdly, even as the World Bank declared in 2002 that in Russia market economy was emerged, under Putin's presidency what has emerged in Russia was State Capitalism. This is because Vladimir Putin reversed several policy decisions of Boris Yeltsin and increased the share of the state over the assets and control of the state over the economy and centralisation of political power. In the 1990's Russia was facing threats for its security and stability due to ethnic violence in Chechnya, Dagestan and many other parts of the country. Hence Putin's had justification for centralising power for consideration of political expediency and preventing the country from falling apart. But on economic front, there was no justification for excessive control over private sector activities.

Fourthly, Russia had not evolved a competitive market economy. On the other hand, state control had increased under Putin's presidency. In fact, a major cause of economic crisis was high level of state control and bureaucratic interference. As opined by some analysts this interference was "facilitated" by excessive administrative barriers where a company's operations, as well as the implementation of its investment plans, were made dependent on the position of particular government officials, who might have interests with the company's rivals. Similar problems arose with regard to procedures for purchasing goods and services for state and municipal needs. High level of bureaucratic control over the economic institutions was a major cause affecting the growth and efficiency of economy. Similarly, foreign investors were particularly affected by such bureaucratic hurdles and barriers, who would otherwise have invested and promoted modernisation of strategic industries in Russia.

Phase III—From State Capitalism to Market Capitalism — Impact of Global Financial Crisis and Recovery

In May 2008, Dmitri Medvedev took over the presidency of Russia being handpicked by Putin, who has also remained in power as prime minister and exerting command over political and economic developments in the country. Both the leaders having close long term association by virtue of being colleagues and hailing from same city St. Petersburg, there was continuity in policies. Being hit by global financial crisis, the leadership was struggling to control economic damage as Russia was once again plunged into declining phase of economy with GDP below three percent per annum, rising inflation, declining exports, growing labour unrest and so on. The major cause of decline was the sharp decline in oil prices from $ 149 per barrel in 2007 to $ 50 per barrel in the autumn of 2008, for which the country was least prepared. But that adversely affected the economy. Apart from decline in oil prices, there was also decline in the demand for hydrocarbon resources caused by global recession specifically in the economies of the USA, West European countries, which were the major customers of Russian oil and gas. Russia has been dependent on the energy sector for its economic development as it accounts for about two-thirds of export earnings.

The impact of economic crisis has been felt on industrial enterprises many of which started either laying off workers or were unable to pay wages. Hence unemployment has become one of the major problems facing Russia's small towns and 'Single-industry towns' (also known as mono-cities) which are worst affected. As per official sources in 2009 unemployment shot up to about 10-12 percent of work force. Apart from private enterprises, state-owned units including large enterprises were also affected. For instance, in 2009 state-owned Russian Railways slashed 54,000 jobs; the steel giant Severstal laid off 9,500 people; automaker GAZ factory slashed 7,500 jobs. Middle and lower income population were the worst hit by crisis. The percentage of people below subsistence minimum was 20-25 percent of the total population living mainly in small towns and rural areas. Workers in several parts of Russia went on strikes and in Buryatia Republic they went on hunger strike in 2009.

In 2009, under the then prevailing domestic and international economic conditions finance minister Alexei Kudrin opined that Russia would experience a difficult next three years as it sought to resolve all the problems accumulated during and after the global economic downturn. In fact, among the BRIC (Brazil, Russia, India and China) countries, Russia was the worst affected and there was genuine concern about economic growth. But fortunately Russian economy passed through the phase of decline and started recovering since 2010. But the recovery has been slow and by the middle of 2011 Russian economy had recovered only by 66 percent of the level it had reached before the latest financial crisis. This is partly due to the trend that prevailed in many European countries. Moreover, in Russia economic recovery retarded and became a challenge because in 2010 Russia's agricultural sector faced the worst drought and heat wave in 130 years due to which production of potatoes declined by over 25 percent and grain production declined to 61 million tons as against 97 million tons in 2009. Considering problems of outdated machinery etc. facing this sector the government has proposed to provide about 130 billion rubles in 2012 for modernising this sector. There are signs of improvement since grain harvest for 2011 is expected to be about 92 million tons. V/ith local consumption of about 70 million tons Russia hopes to export about 20 million tons of grain. Apart from that some policy measures have been taken as a part of social benefit. For instance, on its part the government has taken some measures to reduce the burden by increasing salary by about 10-12 percent and in 2011 average salary increased to 39,700. But due to rising inflation of about 12-15 percent majority of citizens were able to meet expenses of only essential items such as bread, vegetables, coffee etc. Real disposable income declined even though many home pay increased marginally.

As economy showed signs of recovery at the end of 2010 there were reports of qualitative shift in Medvedv-Putin tandem since they started advocating different paths of economic development. In essence Putin taking a conservative approach and being influenced by his team of Igor Sechin and 'Siloviki' preferred continuity. Igor Sechin is a powerful deputy prime minister at the heart of Putin's inner circle, who until recently chaired Rosneft which is Russia's oil behemoth Putin gave the signal that his government was making efforts to sustain growth. On the other hand, Medvedev and his Kremlin economic advisor Arkady Dvorkocich and finance minister Aleksei Kudrin prefer progressive approach and are in favour of change in policy with focus on diversification and modernisation of economy. Putin's policy of continuity was based on one theoretical view of maintaining stability. But contrary to that argument, Medvedev contended that it would lead to stagnation. Hence he even indicated the need to reverse some of the policies that were pursued by Putin. While initially there were some different approaches expressed by both the leaders, both the leaders arrived at consensus on major issues of economic development. This is evident from Putin's statement in July 2011 that deep modernisation and innovation were needed for economic and social growth of Russia. In 2011, Putin also floated Popular Front involving not only political parties, but also civil rights groups, human right activists to demonstrate to Russian elite that he is in favour of pluralism by involving diverse groups of people in decision-making process for the country.

At St. Petersburg Economic Forum in June 2011 Medvedev emphasised that changes were being pursued in economic policy in the country. Medvedev has announced setting up hi-tech IT park at Skolkovo near Moscow for bringing finance, technology and cadre from California. He has also stated that Russia has been keeping up its efforts to de-bureaucratise its economy, introduce easier rules for registering investment projects and remove checks and bottlenecks. Putin has also reiterated changes with regard to government policies and invited foreign investors to invest in Russia. Several policies are announced to bring about real market economic system. For instance, Medvedev agreeing with Economic Development Minister Elvira Nabiullina's proposal has ordered regional governments to decide on privatisation of non-core assets by July 2012. In this regard Russian businessman Mikhail Prokhorov who has become politically active has also reminded that the present model of governance has been exhausted and hence the need for privatisation and redistribution of powers between the federal government and regional administrations. Supporting this approach Medvedev has urged that apart from decentralisation of power, self-regulation organisations must replace state regulation of small business. A major proposal has been made that by 2013 the government would privatise ten top state-owned companies including Rosneft, RusHydro, Sberbank, VTB bank, United Grain by selling share held by the state.

But many of these statements are good as policy declarations, but often these are rhetorics because reality is still complex and hard to change. For instance, Damian Secen who is heading financial consultancy stated in February 2011 that international organisations such as the EBRD and World Bank have accumulated liquidity for projects that have not used by Russian agencies for various shortcomings persisting in the country. Hence the task of reviving economy and achieving sustainable growth has not been easy. Equally important is the question whether Russia will succeed in its core objective of transition to competitive market economy. Hence the Russian leaders face some formidable challenges in their task in the years to come.

Firstly, there is widespread corruption in Russia, which is one of major causes preventing economic development. Some of the major cases involving convictions of former ministers and high level officials during the last three years are Sergei Storchak, the former deputy finance minister, Dmitry Dovgy who was prosecutor, who was investigating the case of embezzlement of leading political figures including Storchank. In fact, some of the activists who were exposing corruption have been criminally assaulted by vested groups or elements. This indicates that not much success has been achieved to tackle this menace of corruption.

Secondly, some of the state-control policies pursued by Putin have adversely affected investment climate in Russia. Foreign investors are also concerned about the risk factor in dealing with issues arising out of uncertain state policies and even with local authorities. It was reported that foreign investors have pulled out of the Moscow to St Petersburg road due to the local protest in 2010. Some foreign companies considered that it was too risky to invest in Russia's struggling infrastructure, which needed huge investment. What is worse even as Russia is seeking foreign capital for recovery, Rossiiskaya Gazeta published in July 2011 the list of 600 individuals and companies involved in money laundering and terrorism financing. The fact that there is still capital flight persisting in the country only served to demonstrate to foreign investors that the 'locals' were not fully convinced about growth prospects and investment risk in Russia although there are also reports of increase in FDI. At any rate getting foreign investment is a challenge for the government for sustained economic development.

Thirdly, apart from lack of resources, there are also institutional constraints and non-tariff barriers. Small, medium and large scale enterprises in private sector have faced the brunt of official and unofficial hurdles including bureaucratic inconsistency, weak rule of law, corruption and outright restrictions in lucrative sectors such as energy. Moreover, Russia's strong bureaucratic structure has expanded significantly during the last decade, which prefers status quo and will be averse to change. Hence any systemic changes desired and proposed by the leadership could be scuttled by the bureaucracy.

Fourthly, even though there is considerable progress made in the process of Russia's integration into the global economy. Russia's much delayed entry into WTO has become a challenge. The delay has been partly political since some former Soviet era republics including Georgia and Baltic States objected to Russia's membership. Apart from that Russia has been facing resistance by some Western countries which are adamant for compliance with conditions and accusing trade restrictive policies pursued by Russia. Notwithstanding these constraints there are strong indications that Russia might join WTO in the near future.

From the above account it is clear that during the last two decades, Russia has passed through different phases of economic development in its objective to bring about systemic changes from communism to market capitalism. The path of transition has not been smooth and it is also marked by reversals of policies. Moreover, the process has been painful for the large section of Russian society. With few months left for parliamentary election to be held in December 2011 and presidential election in March 2012, the present leadership of Medvedev and Putin faces multiple formidable challenges to retain and consolidate their Candem and also to achieve high sustainable economic growth in the years to come.

2

Boris Yeltsin's Controversial Legacy

The recent death of Boris Yeltsin drew varied and contradictory assessments of his tenure as the first president of the Russian Republic after the break-up of the Soviet Union. While western leaders uniformly extolled him as a democrat, in his own country many remembered his mistakes.

Boris Yeltsin, the first president of the independent Russian Republic died at the age of 76 years on April 24, 2007 due to heart failure. The president of Russia Vladimir Putin whom Yeltsin chose as his successor on December 31, 1999 was generous in paying tribute to the former president. He said that under Yeltsin "a new era began and a new democratic Russia was born". He also declared April 25, 2007 as the day of mourning for the departed leader who was buried in Moscow's Novodevichy cemetry, where writer Anton Chekhov and former Soviet leader Nikita Khruschev are also buried. Mikhail Gorbachev, the last president of the former USSR who attended the funeral was more objective and restrained when he stated "... Yeltsin leaves behind him great deeds to the benefit of his country and serious mistakes". In contrast, several leaders of western countries including the former president of the US George Bush Sr, Bill Clinton and others paid rich tributes to Yeltsin for his contribution of bringing democracy and freedom to the Russians and for ending the cold war era. Many western analysts and leaders including John Major of the UK praised Yeltsin as a revolutionary, a reformer and a democratic leader. The western countries had reason to be grateful to Yeltsin for contributing to the dissolution of the Soviet Union and for ending the hold of the Communist Party of the Soviet Union.

There was mixed response in the Russian media to Yeltsin's death. For instance, Moscow'*s Nezavisimaya Gazeta* reported that Yeltsin gave Russians new life and opportunities. But at the same time it criticised him for his blunders. A report by the *RIA Novosti* was Indid in stating that Yeltsin was responsible for the emergence of oligarchs and that his privatisation policy did not benefit the country but brought fortunes for a few Kremlin-connected businessmen. *Moskovsky Komsomolets* wrote that Russia can forgive Yeltsin for his drinking but his privatisation process and war in Chechnya ruined his reputation. *Kommersdnt,* which is generally critical of the Russian government and its policies has been sceptical of Yeltsin's choice of successor stating that "... return to the past is possible".

Some analysts have described Yeltsin as a democrat, courageous, brave, a revolutionary leader, who brought freedom to his people and ended the cold war era. But on the other hand, there are critics who have called him an opportunist, impulsive, erratic and a leader lacking a vision for his country. Thus, Yeltsin who was in office as the president of the Russian Republic from 1991 to 1999 has left a contradictory legacy and in the context of Russian history he has been both an anomaly and atypical leader.

The Rise

Yeltsin was admired for his courageous act in dealing with the coup by a section of communist leaders in August 1991 against the Soviet president Mikhail Gorbachev. Yeltsin stood on the tank in the Red Square in Moscow mobilising a section of the army and his ardent supporters, staring down those involved in the coup. The coup failed and Yeltsin's popularity shot up both at home and abroad. But the same Yeltsin was responsible for resorting to firing on the unarmed and elected body of the Russian Parliament in 1993, which was a shocking and shameful incident.

Those who argue that Yeltsin was an opportunist point out that it was the president of the former USSR Mikhail Gorbachev who brought

Yeltsin from the Siberian oblast of Sverdlovsk to Moscow in 1985 and also inducted him into the politburo the most powerful organ of the Communist Party of the Soviet Union to strengthen the party and the country. But Yeltsin took this opportunity to enhance his own image and political status in the country, which later helped him to become the first president of the independent Russian Republic in 1991. Similarly, as there was growing dissent in the Baltic Republics against the centre, a delegation from the Estonian Republic visited Moscow on August 24, 1991 and approached Yeltsin. Though he was only the president of the Russian Republic, he signed a document recognising the independence of Estonia. Officially it was only the Supreme Soviet of the USSR and president of the USSR Gorbachev who had the authority to sign such a document of independence. Ultimately Gorbachev recognised independence on September 6, 1991. In fact, even the US re-recognised the independence of the Baltic Republics only in September 1991. This is significant because it shows that Yeltsin did not adhere to legal norms. Moreover, he later took the opportunity of the independence of the Baltic Republics from the Soviet Union to convene the meeting of the presidents of Russia, Ukraine and Byelorussia to declare their independence from the Soviet Union, which shocked the world as it virtually amounted to and precipitated the break-up of the USSR.

In the western countries Yeltsin has been hailed as a democrat and a reformer. But many Russian analysts do not subscribe to this assessment because of his several undemocratic actions. According to Russian analyst Boris Nikolaevich, Yeltsin rewrote the constitution of the country to suit his own interest and did not follow the due process of law. Similarly, he was impulsive in taking the hasty decision of starting the first Chechen war in 1994, which was virtually lost. Hence analysts both in Russia and in the west said that often Yeltsin was ruthless and behaved not like a true democrat but like a czar. It is pointed out that in the early period of his presidency, Yeltsin tried to follow the policy of decentralisation of power in the true spirit of democracy. However, under the prevailing conditions in Russia only some resource-rich regions and autonomous republics were benefited. Similarly, Yeltsin promoted freedom of press and speech, which led to the growth of many independent papers and TV channels. But there are disagreements with this assessment. For instance, it is argued that the seeds of individual freedom were already sown by Gorbachev through his policy of Perestroika and Glasnost and that Yeltsin only pursued it.

Yeltsin was re-elected as the president of Russia in 1996, when he defeated his rival from the Communist Party. The western analysts thus observed that he was a truly democratically elected leader. Russian analysts give a different interpretation. According to some of them, at that time a general opinion was created by vested groups in the country that only Yeltsin's leadership alone would help Russia to bail out and prevent the return of the communists and to the Soviet past. They also pointed out that the 1996 election was not totally fair since financial groups used their money power to ensure Yeltsin's victory for their own benefit. In fact, power got concentrated in Kremlin and in the hands of a few individuals such as Berezovsky and Gussinsky who were close to him. Moreover, Yeltsin is also being criticised because while he dismantled former institutions he failed to create new ones. He was impulsive and often inconsistent in his policies, which affected his power and authority. Similarly, Yeltsin also changed prime ministers very often possibly to cover up his own failures in domestic policies and partly to prevent a competitor from appearing on the scene.

Big Disasters, Small Triumphs

Yeltsin's addiction to alcohol often affected his functioning as the head of the nation. As a result of this, on several occasions he was so drunk that he could not show up for meetings with international leaders. Often he was not able to express himself clearly when he appeared on the TV, which damaged his status and reputation both at home and abroad. Some western scholars point out that Yeltsin was the only Russian leader who gave up power voluntarily in a true democratic spirit. But the fact is that he was virtually incapable of discharging his functions and hence handed over the reins of the country to his protege Vladimir Putin.

Many western analysts have appreciated Yeltsin for undertaking the policy of economic liberalisation and building a market economy after the Soviet break-up. Several international financial institutions including the World Bank and the IMF also extended support for his policies. But according to many Russian experts, Yeltsin miserably failed in his economic policies since he was in a greal hurry to bring about transition from the centralised communist economy to capitalist-oriented economy when the situation was not conducive. This is evident in the case of his policy of "Shock Therapy" under which prices were liberalised overnight and state property was privatised leading to economic crisis of unprecedented magnitude during the years 1992 to 1995. His hasty economic policy decisions led to hyperinflation, sharp decline in the gross domestic product and per capita income, large-scale unemployment and so on. The policy of privatisation of state assets even before their valuation was a disaster since it was exploited by a small section of young industrial managers and party apparatchiks who amassed wealth at the cost of a large section of the society including workers. In a short period of five to six years Russian society was polarised into the super rich and the very poor. A class of super rich known as "New Russians", oligarchs and financial mafia groups was created, millionaires who were driving on the Moscow streets in the latest imported cars while a large section of society was impoverished, begging or selling cigarettes and their pets on the streets of Moscow for survival. According to a Russian economist, while the young generation of Russia benefited slightly from Yeltsin's economic policies, the older generation, which had sacrificed their life with the hope of building a new society was driven to destitution and poverty losing their life savings overnight. The reaction of common citizens, therefore, was evident in Yeltsin's popularity rate plummeting to three percent when he relinquished his office at the end of 1999. Yeltsin's failures in economic and social policies led to sharp increase in crime, corruption, prostitution and the mortality rate.

In the matter of foreign policy Yeltsin was oriented more towards the west and he even neglected the east (at least in the initial years) including the Central Asian countries, China and India. Only later was the former prime minister Yevgenii Primakov able to correct this imbalance. Yeltsin was possibly under the impression that with the break-up of the Soviet Union, Russia under his leadership would be immediately embraced by the west as an equal partner. But according to a Russian analyst, Yeltsin became a puppet in the hands of the west and he did as he was told in return for the financial handout. The leading western countries and international financial institutions did support Yeltsin's Russia with liberal financial assistance, but it did not enjoy equal status.

Yeltsin changed world history at the end of the twentieth century. He was admired by the west and disliked by a majority of his own countrymen. Yeltsin's failures far outweighed his achievements as he sought power without the requisite vision and purpose and perhaps was the wrong man at the wrong time for Russia.

3

Refurbishing the Military Industrial Complex

In the context of the numerous accidents involving Russian-made MiG aircraft in India, it is interesting to examine how the military industrial complex, which had disintegrated after the collapse of the Soviet Union is being remodelled and refurbished and the challenges it faces. The upgradation and modernisation programme and the promotion of R and D appear to be leading to a re-emergence of Russia as a major producer and exporter of arms in the world lagging behind only the US.

The frequency with which Russia made MiG -21s have crashed in the recent past has given them a bad reputation of being called the 'flying coffins'. The record of crashes is indeed alarming. According to press reports, three MiG-21s, three MiG-23s and one Jaguar have crashed between January and June 2003 *(The Times of India,* July 18, 2003). One Category-I aircraft accident has taken place almost every 17 days. Since 1991, 306 Category-I accidents have taken place taking a toll of the precious lives of 150 pilots. It is estimated that every time a fighter crashes, the loss could be around Rs 3 crore to Rs 100 crore possibly including millions of rupees spent on training the pilots.

The crash of MiGs assumes significance because all the different variants of MiGs taken together constitute 75 percent of the IAF combat fleet. MiGs are reported to be 'fully air-worthy' which implies that accidents have taken place mainly due to 'human error' - inadequate flying skills, judgment errors, lack of situational awareness and inability to cope with technical defects and so on. On the other hand, it is opined by some analysts that bad maintenance practices and poorly manufactured spares could have possibly contributed to the crashes. According to Anil Gadgil, a former Indian Air Force pilot, currently with Air India and father of Abhijit, a pilot who lost his life in a MiG-21 crash in 2001 "...MiGs-21s belonged to a vintage era, its spares were a problem and the pilots did not have adequate training".

The issue of MiG should also be viewed in the general context of India's defence capability and preparedness. During the last few decades a major part of India's overall defence equipment needs have been met from the former Soviet Union and from the post-Soviet Russia not only for the Air Force but also for the army and the navy by procuring Russian T-90S main battle tanks, warships and so on. However, there were press reports (*The Times of India,* July 28, 2003) to the effect that the Russian T 90 battle tanks have developed technical snags within a few months after being inducted into the Indian army. The Russian team, however, was rectifying the technical snags. Similarly, the Indian Navy may soon induct INS Talwar and INS Trishul multipurpose stealth frigates with sophisticated weaponry from Russia. India may decide to procure the much discussed and debated billion dollar worth retired Russian ship Admiral Gorshkov which is being re-equipped possibly with MiGs. Cooperation in the defence sector was an important component in building strategic partnership between India and the former USSR, which has been sustained and strengthened by India in recent years. But since more than a decade has passed after the Soviet break-up, it may be worthwhile to examining the state of the military industrial complex (MIC) of Russia.

After taking over the presidency of Russia in the year 2000, Vladimir Putin made an important statement that Russia's MIC was archaic and that it did not correspond to contemporary military-political tasks of the country. In fact, Putin's views on the state of the MIC were based on the assessment of the heads of Russia's defence establishments. In an interview published on August 18,1999 in Russia's defence journal *Krasnaya Zvezda* (Red Star), General Anatoli

Kornukov, the commander-in-chief of the Russian Air Force stated that the aging of the fleet was 'Number 1 Headache' for Russia's air force. He opined that due to the lack of funding, the number of fighter planes had fallen from several thousands a decade back to a few hundred by 1999. Only half of the planes under his command, he said, could be described as modern. What was more alarming is his opinion that the survival of Russia's air force depended on its ability to sell used aircrafts, rent out airfields and providing commercial transport. The situation did not improve much because *Nezavisimaya Gazeta* (Independent Journal) reported on the February 11, 2002 that one of the reasons for young officers leaving the defence service was the poor condition of military equipment which was particularly the case with the Russian air force which had very few new aircrafts and helicopters over the past decade.

The situation was no better in the Russian navy. According to an article in *Nezavisimoe Voennoe Obozrenie* (Independent Military Review) No. 30 of 2000, more and more ships were falling into disrepair for lack of funds. Hence if that situation continued, then by 2010 Russian navy would have only 100 ships of all classes. As stated by Fleet Admiral Vladimir Kuroedov, the commander of the Russian Navy (*KrasnayaZvezda,* January 6, 2003), the Russian navy decided to scrap one-fifth of its ships due to the shortage of funds. He said that since 1995, the navy had been receiving only 12 percent of funding it needed for maintenance.

There are a few other aspects concerning the archaic nature of the Russian MIC. According to Goskomstat (State Statistical Committee) report of 2001, as of 1999, 78 percent of the machinery and equipment in the MIC enterprises to produce armaments was more than 10 years old and about 35 percent of machinery was over 20 years old. In fact, Putin himself had stated in 1999 that only 20 percent of MIC plants were functioning and that many were to be closed down. Moreover, Putin was also unhappy with the organisational aspects of the MIC. Speaking at the meeting of the Security Council devoted to the mobilisation of the Russian armed forces, he remarked in November 1999 that Russia's mobilisation procedures were outdated and they did not correspond with the prevailing political and economic realities. He added that while Russia had abandoned central economic planning, it continued to use the old, inefficient and unreliable system of military management for dealing with emergency situations.

Production Trends in MIC

According to Russian statistical sources, against the base of 1991, the index of overall production of the MIC enterprises declined to about 46 percent in 2001. The trend in production during the last decade shows two distinct phases. The first phase comprises the period from 1991 to 1998 and the second from 1998 to 2001. The production declined by about between 1991 and 1998. Subsequently, there has been a steady increasing trend, Moreover, even in the first phase, during 1991-1994 the fall in defence production was particularly drastic, which indicated that the severity of the immediate impact of the Soviet break-up in 1991. The enterprises of the MIC produced both arms and defence equipment and also a wide range of items for civilian needs as was the case during the Soviet period. Moreover, the policy of conversion of defence industries into civilian economy has also been pursued after the Soviet break-up. Hence examining these data, it is important to note that the decline in the production of defence equipment was more pronounced than that of civilian production. Thus, in 2001, the output of defence equipment was below 18 percent as compared to the level of 1991, while in the case of civilian output the index was over 33 per cent. However, the overall trend with regard to the two phases has been quite similar in both the cases and that output levels reached the lowest levels by 1997-1998 and subsequently there has been some modest increase in production.

During the years 1999 and 2000, less than five percent of the machinery in the MIC was less than five years old, while over 75 percent was more than 10 years old. Also, about one-third of machinery in the MIC of Russia was more than 20 years old, which shows the extent to which the machinery had become outdated. In a sense the situation in the MIC was not much different from that in the engineering industry as a whole. In the 2000 about 85 percent of machinery and equipment in Russia was more than 10 years old. Partly, the lack of investment was because domestic demand for defence equipment had gone down as a result of which capacity utilisation of machinery in the MIC sector was as low as 17 percent in 1997. However, export market for Russian defence machinery and equipment improved particularly since in the mid-1990s.

One reason for this state of affairs was that Russia's foreign policy under Boris Yeltsin's leadership particularly in the initial period was strongly pro-western and the foreign minister Andrei Kozyrev was keen to bring Russia closer to the US at any cost. It was argued that the threat perception that prevailed in the bygone era of superpower rivalry had vanished. Hence some policy-makers opined that priority given in the past to the MIC had become irrelevant. Russia also initiated the process of economic reforms of in which market conditions, competition, quality, price, etc, were important considerations. Industrial enterprises including those in the MIC were not yet adjusted to these market conditions and hence their production was affected being unable to compete with goods imported liberally from abroad. This was particularly the case in respect of enterprises of the MIC, which under the policy of conversion, were also producing civilian goods. Moreover, with the breakup of the Soviet Union, economic linkages that prevailed in the past among various enterprises of the MIC located in different republics of the former USSR were broken. In fact, this was a serious problem for all other sectors of the economy as well and almost all the newly independent countries suffered in maintaining their economic activities to varying degrees.

Putin's Policy of MIC

Vladimir Putin has initiated several policy measures to enable the MIC to overcome the years of neglect. Firstly, an important policy initiated by Putin was to reduce the size of the MIC by emphasising quality rather than quantity. This policy was spelt out by the then deputy prime minister of Russia Ilya Klebanov in July 2001 when he stated that nearly half of the size of the MIC was to be reduced over a period of five years. Some of the MIC units were to completely change their focus from defence to civilian goods production. The policy of reducing the size of the MIC was in a sense linked to the reform and restructuring of the MIC. Thus, for instance, 2,000-odd defence-related enterprises were to be combined into 50 major structures through consolidation and amalgamation of non-viable and unprofitable units into viable units. The former ministry dealing with the military industrial organisation has been converted into federal defence agency. Thus, at present the Russian MIC has 15 branches, the most important among them are - Russian Avia-Cosmos Agency; Aviation Industry; Russian Agency for Space Administration; Radio Industry; Electronic Industry and so on. In 2001 two branches, namely, the Russian Avia-Cosmos Agency and the Russian Agency for Systems Management have played a dominant role accounting for about 72 percent of all MIC enterprises and they accounted for about 60 percent of output as well as employment. The Avia-Cosmos Agency has 414 enterprises out of which 306 are engaged in the manufacture of a wide range of aviation products including fighter planes such as MiGs, Sukhoi, etc. So far as the aviation branch is concerned, 17 conglomerates were to be formed which would specialise in the production of missiles and space hardware. The Russian state, however, will hold 51 percent of shares in all defence holdings. These units have reportedly contributed a great deal to the revival of Russia's MIC.

Putin has also initiated the process of modernising the MIC. Importance has been given to the aviation branch of the MIC, which accounted for about 30 percent of Russia's defence sector and about 60 percent of exports in 2001. Modernisation and upgradation has been considered necessary to keep pace with the advancement in this sector and meeting the growing competition in the world market. Hence Vladimir Babek, a spokesman for the Sukhoi aircraft company announced in January 2001 that the Sukhoi firm was finalising the upgradation and modernisation of Su-25 ground attack planes. The first 100 Su-25 were to be modernised by 2008 for meeting the needs of the Russian air force. An equal number of Sukhoi planes were to be modernised for foreign customers. In the opinion of Russia's defence expert Vladimir Komarov, all these measures were intended with a view to develop Russia's MIC along the lines of NATO operation in Yugoslavia and provide Russia's armed forces with modern high precision weapons.

All these policy measures and practical efforts undertaken by the Russian government as well as by the heads of MIC units during the last few years have enabled major enterprises of the MIC to expand their levels of output, many of which produce high quality defence items. In fact, many MIC units have emerged as important producers among the major arms manufacturers in the world. Thus, according to the US magazine, (*Defense News* No. 32 in 2001), a half-dozen Russian defence companies are represented on its list of the 100 leading global weapon producers. The Russian group is headed by Rosvoor-uzhenie, which ranks 13th with revenues of $ 3.09 billion; Sukhoi in 35th place with $ 900 million; Severnaya Verf in 52nd place with $ 532 million; Antei in 62nd place with $ 350 million; MiG in 88th place with $ 100 million; and Tula Rifles Works in 90th place with $ 90 million. Thus, after a decade of the Soviet disintegration, the Russian policy-makers have reason to be happy that many enterprises of the MIC have regained their position as leading weapon producers in the world.

Advancement in R and D

While some branches of the MIC were in pathetic condition, Russian scientists and engineers did make some achievements in specific branches of the R and D of the MIC. According to the ministry of defence spokesperson in September 2001, Russia developed a new supersonic antitank missile 'Vikhir' which was capable of piercing upto 1000 millimetres of armour. Similarly, Russia started manufacturing the KAB-500Kr smart bombs, which were claimed to be without parallel in the world. According to Russian defence experts, this new bomb is based on television honing devices with a correlational target data processing algorithm to land precisely on target. According to Russian sources, one defence enterprise started producing a new supersonic cruise missile the X-22M, which has a range of 400 km and a speed of 3,600 km per hour.

A new aspect in R and D in Russia's MIC has been the growing collaboration with some of the western countries in developing new products intended for both military as well as civilian needs. For instance, the CEO of Russia's Sukhoi aircraft company Mikhail Pogosyan stated in August 2002 that his corporation in a joint venture activity with the US firm Boeing and the Russian firm Ilyushin have created a new fleet of jets consisting of 55-seat, 75-seat and 95-seat airplanes with a flight range of 3,500-6,000 km. This new aircraft would be ready for flight testing by 2004 and already a dozen companies seemed to have shown their interest in this new plane. In June 2003, Russia and France have proposed to develop the fifth generation aircraft to meet future needs in the civil aviation sector. Similarly, Gagarin Aircraft Manufacturing Association based in Khabarovsk-On-Amur in Russia's Far-East has developed a new model of the BE-103 executive amphibian plane which is equipped with the US made engines. This plane can reportedly fly at a speed of 300 km. It has a flight range of 1,000 km and is an ideal choice for airlifting people and cargo to remote locations. An added advantage of this plane is that it does not require runaways and can land on water and snow. The spokesman of this factory claims that this new plane has obtained national and international flight certificates. Considering these multiple advantages, which can meet military and civilian needs, this plane is expected to have great demand in international markets. From the above account it appears that there is a glaring contrast between the archaic conditions in some part of the MIC while Russian scientists have made great advancement with regard to R and D in a few specific branches of this sector.

Exports by MIC Sector

After the Soviet break-up, there was sharp decline in the quantum of domestic demand. Under the prevailing chaotic conditions, exports of the MIC also declined in the early 1990s. But subsequently many of the organisations of the MIC started making conscious efforts to concentrate on export as a means of survival. After 1994-95 exports of the MIC started picking up significantly contributing to the revival of this sector. In fact, the defence equipments of the MIC and oil-gas resources of the energy sector were two main sources of exports from Russia that have helped the country to earn much needed hard currency.

Considering the vital role that the MIC has played in the country, Putin has given further encouragement to this sector by signing a decree in September 2000, which opened the door for freer arms trade from the country. The decree defined in particular, the types of military equipments and systems that were available for exports and countries to which such defence related materials could be exported. The underlying objective was that there was no need for the government approval on a case-by-case basis that was necessary in the past (*VremyNovostei,* September 4, 2000). This policy declaration gave further boost for exports. By 1995-96, Russia's rank in the world improved but still lagged behind Britain and France. By 1999 with expected arms exports of about $ 6 billion, the deputy prime minister, Ilya Klebanov claimed that Russia was to surpass Britain and France. In 2000, as per the US Congressional Research Report, Russia exported $ 7.7 billion worth of arms trailing behind only the US, which exported arms worth $ 18.6 billion out of the total world arms export of $ 36.9 billion. This shows the rapid increase in arms exports by Russia during the last few years.

Among the various branches of the MIC, the aviation group made tremendous progress on the export front accounting for nearly two-third of exports in the year 2000. China has been the major customer of Russian fighter planes. For instance, in the year 2001, the Sukhoi aviation company delivered 50 jet fighters to clients out of which China bought 40 Sukhoi jet fighters. From this it appears that the Chinese leaders have shown preference for Sukhoi to other fighters in its policy to upgrade and modernise its air force. From its long experience of using Soviet fighter planes, it is possible that China's defence experts might have considered Sukhoi fighter planes to be safer and effective than say MiGs, a matter which deserves to be looked into by India's policy-makers. Another significant aspect of China's procurement of defence equipments is that according to Alexei Arbatov, a Duma member and academic, China has been the largest buyer of Russia's state-of-the-art conventional armaments, which are lacking even within the Russian army. Moreover, China has acquired even the licensing rights to manufacture them (Andrei Arbatov 'What Kind of Army Does Russia Need' in the journal *Russia in Global Affairs,* Moscow, Vol. 1, No. 1 Jan-Mar 2003, p. 78). A western analyst has aptly commented that while Russia has been helping China's rise as a global power, Chinese cash keeps Russian industries afloat.

Besides China, India, Iran, Iraq, Libya are other traditional markets for Russia's arms exports. Russia has made successful efforts to sell hi-tech weapons to new markets in south-east Asia. For instance, Malaysia has taken keen interest to purchase Su-30 fighters,

T-90 tanks and obtain licences to manufacture the Igla air defence missiles. Similarly, Indonesia, which faced US embargo on the purchase of military supplies in 2002, wants to purchase Russian planes including Su-30 for modernising its air force. The Russian daily newspaper *Izvestiya* reported on July 31, 2002 that Russia was planning to sell over a period of 10 years up to 500 aircraft at the cost of $ 17 billion. How Russia has been serving its own national interest can be understood from the fact that Russia will be getting concessions and licensing rights in Indonesia's mining and other natural resource extraction sectors in exchange for the sale of arms. So far as Indonesia is concerned, apart from overcoming the problem of US embargo, Russia's military equipment are found to be cheaper than that from the US. At any rate all these efforts have enabled the Sukhoi enterprise to emerge as one of the leading arms manufacturers in the world. In fact, as reported by *Moscow Times,* December 27, 2001, the chief of Sukhoi firm Mikhail Pogosyan claimed that 2001 was the best year since the Soviet collapse. Not to lag behind aviation firms, naval units of the MIC have stepped up efforts to export defence equipment. Vladimir Pospelov, the director of the Russian government's shipbuilding agency stated in October 2002 that in 2003 shipbuilders expect to surpass aircraft plants in arms sales as reported by ITAR-TASS on the October 1, 2002. It could be that Pospelov might have expected that among other contracts, the agreement on the sale of Admiral Gorshkov to India might bring in mighty dividends.

Russia has ventured to sell arms to some European countries as well. The prime minister of Russia Mikhail Kasynov during his visit to Austria in January 2002, was exploring the possibility of selling MiG-29 fighters and also construct a factory in Austria to produce MiG-110 business-class jets. It is interesting to note that through these aviation deals, Russia proposes to repay its $ 28 billion Soviet era debt to Austria rather than paying in hard currency.

Russia's policy-makers are introducing some new methods with regard to the organisation and operation of arms exports. For instance, Rosorbornexport (Russia's arms exporting organisation) and Russia's oil producing company Lukoil have entered into an agreement to promote each other's interest in foreign markets. Thus, Lukoil will help arms sales in countries where the oil giant already has an established market presence. In turn, Rosorbornexport will give concessions in the oil sector of the national governments in which it is involved *(Profil,* Moscow No. 34, 2002). Similarly, with increasing quantum of arms exports and huge amount of money involved, Rosorbornexport proposes to convert itself from being a mere trade mediator in arms to investment agency for Russia's MIC. In the opinion of the general director of Rosorbornexport, "a state mediator lacking its own production base is at the risk of being exposed to various fluctuations and can simply not survive" (*Vedomosti,* November 26, 2001). Thus, Rosorbornexport is seeking to increase its stake in the Sukhoi aircraft holding company which accounts for more than 50 percent of exports from Russia.

There is another interesting development with regard to arms exports from Russia. Among the former Soviet republics, besides Russia, Ukraine had been an important producer and exporter of arms. After years of difficulties, Ukraine has again emerged as an important arms producing and exporting country. Presumably considering this development, Rosorbornexport has signed an agreement with Ukrspetsexport (Ukrainian State-owned defence trading organisation), to boost arms sales of both Russia and Ukraine. According to reports available from Russia, the arrangement seems to jointly market the sales of 'similar defence equipment' to the third countries and even undertake their joint production. In short, Rosorbornexport wants to avoid competition and price cuts by each other so that both the organisations can maximise their profits on arms sales to third countries. Russia has also entered into an arrangement for closer cooperation in the production and export of defence items with five other CIS countries, namely, Byelorus, Kazakhstan, Tajikistan. Kyrgyzstan and Armenia. All these measures may help Putin's Russia to reestablish its status and influence in international, political and security-related issues.

Challenges

Russia continues to face certain serious problems and challenges. One such relates to the condition of the defence personnel. Deteriorating condition of the MIC during the years after the Soviet disintegration affected the living conditions of the armed forces. During the Soviet era, defence personnel were receiving goods and various benefits such as subsidised housing, education, etc. With financial constraints facing the country, many of these benefits were not offered. The worst affected were the young Russian soldiers who returned to Russia from the East European countries after the dissolution of the Warsaw Pact and from other Soviet republics. Many of them did not possess requisite higher qualification or any technical skills to be able to easily get employment under changing conditions in the country. The situation has persisted over the years. According to an article published in *Vek,* No. 25, 2000 only 10 percent of military personnel received all goods and benefits to which they were entitled. This has worsened the living conditions of a large number of soldiers who are living below poverty line. The resource crunch has been quite serious which is evident from the fact that according to Russian press reports the salaries were not paid regularly to soldiers in several regions of the country. The Russian paper *Nazavisimaya Gazeta* reported on February 11, 2002 that since 1991 over 40,000 officers had quit military service. The main reasons for such large exodus of officers from military service were - low salaries, inadequate social conditions, lack of status, and hazardous technical equipment. As a result of this, about 10 percent of medium rank officers and about 30 percent of petty officer positions were vacant. Equally important is the fact that salary levels of even middle rank officers in the defence service were quite low at about 5,000 rubles ($ 200), which made them quit army service for much higher level of salary in the civilian economy. The commander-in-chief of Russia's armed forces Nikolai Kormiltsev stated in January 2002 that a large number of officers had left the ranks to join private service in the country. Those who stayed were to work under very hard conditions particularly in Dalnevostochnii (Par Eastern) and Sibiriskii (Siberian) military districts.

Beating of soldiers by officers and by fellow soldiers is another problem affecting personnel in Russia's military services. According to a report of September 9, 2001, Soldiers Mothers' Committee stated that as many as 30,000 army soldiers were beaten and hence over 15,000 soldiers and their parents appealed to the Committee for assistance. Considering the repetition of such incidents, in April 2003 the committee sent a letter to the defence minister demanding that an enquiry committee be sent to the Birobidzan garrison to investigate the hazing and harassment allegations. All these have made a serious impact on the willingness of the young men to join military service. In the opinion of major general Yuri Smetana, the deputy chief of staff of the Moscow military district, in July 2002 about 25,000 draftees refused to serve when they were called up for service. Low salary, poor social conditions, hazing, etc., seem to have led to the problem of desertion that the Russian military has been facing on a growing scale. As reported by *Novaya Izvestiya* on October 5, 2002, these deserters hide for years and even use violence against those seeking to arrest them.

Possibly due to all these factors according to a secret poll held among the military personnel in 2001, Putin was losing his popularity and influence within the military. Nearly 50 percent of military officers did not support his policies as (*Zavtra,* No. 34, 2001). In order to solve these problems Putin had promised that salaries of soldiers would be revised by early 2003, but this decision seems to have been further postponed. However, in a major policy decision announced in July 2003 to reform the MIC, Putin has proposed free higher educational facilities to be offered to the Russian citizens who will serve in the armed forces for a specific period. The prime minister of Russia Kasyanov stated in October 2001 that the government proposed to spend about $ 35 million over a period of four years to deal with the problem of resettlement of military personnel through re-qualification, etc. It is to be seen how far these policies will help the Russian policy-makers to attract young Russians to attract and retain them in military service.

There is another challenge that the Russian leadership faces and that relates to the fact that criminal groups are getting attracted to the MIC. According to Russian journalist Pavel Felgenhauer who specialises in defence-related issues, the main reason for this growing incidents of crime in the MIC is the high profit potential stemming from lucrative arms deals with foreign countries. The DUMA members have recently protested against the government about this new phenomenon of the penetration by criminal elements in the defence sector, which are resorting to gangland-style of killings. In the first week of June 2003, Igor Klimov, the acting general director of Almaz-Antei and Segei Shchitko, the commercial director of the RATEP defence plant were gunned down in two separate incidents. Almaz-Antei was formed in 2002 by the presidential decree, which manufactures some of the most advanced air-defence systems, such as the S-400 and S-300 anti-aircraft and anti-missile systems, which accounted for exports worth about $ 5-7 billion in 2002. According to some Russian analysts, Klimov was a victim of the power struggle within the organisation since Almaz-Antei's management included rival military groups. It is also reported that Klimov who was appointed recently by Putin, was targeted possibly because some sections of the old guard were afraid of being exposed in earlier transactions involving millions of dollars.

The state of Russia's MIC which supplies a substantial part of military equipment to India has been far from satisfactory. A detailed study needs to be undertaken to examine whether there could be any direct linkage between the state of Russia's MIC and problems facing the IAF in particular and India's defence preparedness in general. There has been some improvement in recent times. Putin has initiated several policy measures during the three years including the downsizing of the MIC; undertaking the task of upgradation and modernisation of machinery to produce armaments; promoting R and D in defence enterprises and organisations and so on. All these measures seem to have given handsome dividends making Russia re-emerge as a major producer and exporter of arms in the world lagging behind only the US.

4

Is Russia's Crackdown on NGOs Justifiable?

In Russia, Non-Government Organisations (NGOs) have been subjected to indiscriminate checking and investigation during the last few months, raising considerable resentment both inside the country and abroad. In the first week of June 2013, Russia has legalised 'Random Checking' of NGOs. This has in fact compounded the problems of those engaged in the civil society movement in the country because prior to this legislation, in November 2012, a law became effective under which any NGO that received money from abroad was required to register as "foreign agent" failing which it could face severe administrative action. Despite massive domestic and international criticism, Vladimir Putin had signed this law in July 2012, that is, within one month of taking over the presidency, having got the full backing of Russia's ruling United Russia party which contended that NGOs in Russia were excessively politicised and financed from abroad and needed to be regulated. Shuvalov, a spokesman of the ruling party, was even frank in stating: "NGOs operated as an instrument of influence on Russia from abroad."

But disagreeing with these contentions, journalists, several members of the Liberal-Democratic Party, Yabloko had protested against the bill that branded NGOs involved in political activity and funded from abroad as "foreign agents". Thus, both these laws have caused deep concern and the NGO community in Russia has been resisting these laws and many, refusing to register' as 'foreign agents' as this new policy measure has increased state control over NGOs and restricted their freedom and activities in the country. Notwithstanding protests, and resentment, by passing these laws, the Russian President has demonstrated his authority over the role of NGOs in the country. Hence this policy measure assumes considerable importance in Russia's social and political life as Putin will remain President of the country till June 2018.

The institution of the NGO is a relatively new phenomenon in independent and democratic Russia during the last about two decades even as there was a dissident movement in the former Soviet Union and a few organisations such as the Rights Organisation of the Moscow Helsinki Group operated in the country. At present officially there are about 650 NGOs in the country engaged in various social, economic and political activities. In view of this it is worthwhile to know why Putin has taken this controversial policy measure, what are the reactions to this policy both in Russia and abroad, what will be the likely impact of this policy and how far he will succeed in his objectives.

There are several possible reasons for the Russian Government initiating such controversial policies. Firstly, Putin's resentment against some NGOs seems to have been caused by the protests against him since 2011 when he announced his decision to contest for presidency for the third term, as permissible, under the Russian Constitution, and subsequently during his campaign for election in April-May 2012. In May 2012, protests against Putin continued even after he was declared, elected and they, were at their peak at the Bolotnaya Square in Moscow as also on the internet. Hence the Russian parliament also passed bills on blacklisting undesirable internet sites which, in turn, have raised concerns about a general clampdown on civil society.

Secondly, from the Russian perception, activities of some NGOs amounted to foreign interference in internal affairs of the country. For instance, a NGO known as 'Golos' (Voice), that is funded substantially by the USA, had been contesting the official claim of fairness in regional and Duma elections in December 2011. Taking advantage of freedom of the press in Russia, Golos had been widely reporting vote-rigging and fraud in elections in Russia and even questioning the popularity and extent of Putin's success in the election. What might have further agitated the Russian Government was that Golos was one of the Russian NGOs that lodged a complaint with the European Court of Human Rights about the "foreign agents" law in February 2013. Hence, as per reports, members of Golos' independent election watchdog Andrei Buzin, Grigory Melkonyants have been tried earlier in Russian courts and are now targeted by the new law on "foreign agent".

Thirdly, while claiming that these laws are not against NGOs per se, the Russian Government has justified that this law is in the national interest and a necessary measure to prevent foreign meddling in Russia's public life. Russian political leader Alexander Sidyakin of the United Russia Party has alleged that an entire network of NGOs operate in Russia whose financing was suspicious from the standpoint of its provider. He has alleged that Golos was paid $ 2 million in 2011 to dirty the Russian authorities. Similarly, in support of this argument and reacting to public protests against these new laws, the Justice' Ministry of Russia has contended that the goal was to check if their activities were in line with the legislation and corresponded with the objectives of their charters. There is tit-for-tat between the USA and Russia on human rights issues. For instance, the USA introduced the Magnitsky Act (Russian lawyer Magnitsky, who was a human rights activist, died in jail in 2009) and imposed sanctions on Russian officials on the issue of human rights violations and in turn Russia responded by banning US citizens from adopting Russian children.

Fourthly, Russian leaders could have some legitimate concern about the role of NGOs in 'Colour Revolutions' that occurred in some former Soviet republics including Ukraine, Georgia, Kyrgyz Republic during the last over a decade causing political instability in these newly independent states. Hence as a preventive measure Russian leaders seem to have introduced this policy to ensure political stability in the country. Russian leaders also seem to contend that support to certain Russian NGOs by some Western countries and institutions was "ideology based" and against the policy and ideology being pursued by Russia including on issues relating to human rights activities. Thus, there are ideological differences between Russia and the West on issues relating to NGOs.

For instance, the European Union has exerted constant pressure on the Russian authorities to meet the OSCE standards on human rights, democracy, rule of law and the independence of the judiciary. But while disagreeing with these views of the European Union on this issue, the Russian Government expressed openness in providing detailed clarifications as to the implementation of the Russian law.

Fifthly, the Russian Government might be legitimately interested to know the exact amount of foreign money and, equally important, the sources of funding received by the NGOs. These new laws will also help the government to indirectly control their financial position apart from knowing as to who is funding. Hence Russian NGOs, that did not comply with the new law, were also subjected to heavy fines. In fact, Golos was the first NGO to face heavy administrative charges and fined $ 10,000 forcing them to abide by the new law that has raised concern in the West. As opined by some civil right activists, the amount of fines are heavy and might force many NGOs to close down and that seems to be the objective of the government. Putin has claimed that Russian NGOs received almost $ 1 billion in foreign funding in 2013. In fact, possibly to counter foreign funding, Putin has offered $ 75 million to NGOs that are working for social causes in Russia dealing with education, health care etc.

Arguments Against the Law

There are several arguments and contentions by those who are protesting against these laws on NGOs. Firstly, the term "foreign agent" has overtones of spying and indeed amounts to treason and discredits an NGO in the eyes of the public. Hence there is considerable resentment among political activists and part of the educated middle class population who support the values of freedom, human rights of a democratic system in their country because branding all NGOs as foreign agents simply because they are getting funding from abroad is totally unacceptable to them. The veteran human rights activist, Lev Ponomaryov, of the For Human Rights Organisation has been very critical and stated that the new law was an attack on the entire Russian civil liberties movement.

Secondly, the term 'foreign agent' to an NGO, as applied by the Russian Government—irrespective whether it receives one percent or 90 percent of its total funds for its activities —and clubbing all such NGOs in one category, does not seem to be rational. Even the issue of source of funding is important since institutions such as the United Nations Organisation do provide funding to NGOs and there is no justification to call all of them as foreign agents. On its part, one possible intention of the Russian Government is to control several Russians who have laundered money during the last two decades and, living abroad, could be funding some NGOs to oppose Putin. Notwithstanding this contention, clubbing all NGOs as 'foreign agents' has created controversy in the country and abroad. There is a legitimate need to differentiate between NGOs based on the source of foreign funding rather than branding all as foreign agents. Moreover, what is important is the nature and functions of activities any NGO is carrying out in the country, political, social or educational.

Thirdly, there could be valid apprehension about the term 'random checking' since as the law is applied in reality it may not be 'random' nor is it 'checking'. There is a strong possibility of targeting certain NGOs. Hence international funding agencies —such as the UNO, Helsinki Foundation, that are funding NGOs —have expressed their concern with random checking and branding NGOs as 'foreign agents', and the manner of investigation by the Russian Government agencies. In fact, many NGOs, including international human rights groups, are critical of the humiliating manner of carrying out unannounced and lengthy inspections by the Russian administrative bodies. This is contrary to the claim of simply checking. Many NGOs allege that inspection by government officials was 'extraordinary' while the Russian Government claimed that it was 'routine'.

In the first week of June 2013, the UN human rights experts expressed their concern that two NGOs, namely, the Centre Memorial in St. Petersburg and the Public Verdict Foundation in Moscow, have been selectively targeted and charged by the Russian authorities. These two organisations seem to have provided information on human rights violations in Russia to the UN Committee Against Torture. In fact, being concerned with Russia's administrative actions, the UNO has sought assurance that these two groups will not have to face any reprisals 'as a result of their legitimate activities'. Thus, antagonising these international agencies and organisations will have an adverse impact on the image of the Russian Government as a democratic country. Hence the Director of Human Rights Watch of Europe, Hugh Williams, has opined that the Russian Government's crackdown on NGOs was hurting Russian society and harming Russia's international standing. What is important to note is that the Human Rights Watch, in its report of 2012, has made critical observations about Russia's performance stating that the Russian 'authorities introduced a series of restrictive laws, harassed and intimidated activists, and interfered in the work of Non-Government Organisations, crushing hopes for reform'.

Fourthly, some NGOs have legitimate concern if they are to be called 'foreign agents'. Hence they have maintained that the law was likely to be misused to put unfair pressure on their activities. Their concern is based on the possibility that it could be used indiscriminately against groups that are engaged in social and humanitarian activities. It is a well-known fact that there are some institutions that are engaged in education and receive funding from abroad. For instance, according to Russian Government prosecutors, during the last one year the Moscow School of Political Studies has received from abroad 12.8 million rubles ($ 411,600) including 7.3 million rubles ($ 235,000) from the US-based Open-Society Foundation, also known as George Soros Foundation. As per Russian law, this institution has to be registered as a foreign agent. This does not appear to be rational since it is engaged in promoting education and research.

Fifthly, accusation of foreign countries and institutions by the Russian Government that by giving financial support to NGOs they are meddling in its internal affairs may not be sustainable and convincing. In Russia, apart from NGOs, many Opposition party leaders have been actively opposing Putin's policies. Therefore, the protest movement in Russia may not be contained by these policy measures aimed at restricting the foreign funding of NGOs.

In lieu of conclusion it may be stated that the Russian President, Vladimir Putin, has reasons to express his anger with the protests against his legitimate election as the President for the third term that has led to the enactment of laws on NGOs. The Russian Governments concerned over the activities of certain NGOs and has some genuine perception about the impact of their activities on the country's political stability. But at the same time both the laws concerning NGOs have created considerable disagreement and controversy in Russia and abroad. There are certain shortcomings in the indiscriminate branding of all NGOs as 'foreign agents' for receiving funding from abroad and the manner in which the random checking law seems to have been applied and implemented in reality. The objective of totally controlling the activities of NGOs and containing protests against these laws in the country and abroad by passing these laws may not be fully achieved. On the other hand, considering the severe adverse reactions both at home and abroad even by the UNO, there is a need and possibility of certain revisions in a bid to modernising the civil code in Russia.

5

Two Decades of Putin's Leadership of Russia: Highlights of Achievements and Challenges

It is important to recall that 31st December 1999 was a historic day as the then Russian president Boris Yeltsin used the occasion not only to convey his New Year Greetings but also to announce his resignation and endorse Vladimir Putin - 47 years old a former KGB officer who had been prime minister since August but who was virtually unknown to the public before 1998— as his successor. He made Putin as acting president and described him as "the man on whom practically every Russian has pinned his hopes for the future," a person "deserving of being president".

Taking over the position as acting president, Putin got duly elected as president with overwhelming majority in March 2000 and has been in power of Russia during the last 20 years, not violating the constitutional provisions, two terms as president and one term as prime minister, current presidency ending in 2024.

It is appreciable that based on data from various sources such as World Bank, United Nations and OECD etc. Russia analyst Kristyna Foltynova has rightly opined by that Putin is dealing with a struggling economy, tough Western sanctions, unpopular government reforms, and a drop in his approval rating. An effort has been made to highlight few achievements and challenges of Putin's leadership.

It needs to be mentioned at the outset that hopes and "expectations of former Russian leaders such as Mikhail Gorbachev and Boris Yeltsin, which was also the aim and intention of Western powers, that Russia will succeed in its transformation from its former Communist system to political democracy and market economy have not materialised. As opined by academics and analysts, even as there are few political parties prevailing in Russia apart from the Communist Party, they have no major role and are mainly on paper. As opined by many analysts, there is centralisation of power in Kremlin as in the past, exercised by Putin over socio-economic and political issues.

To mention a few cases Putin has handled with iron hand on five-day conflict with Georgia in the last decade and annexation of Crimea in 2014 linking Russia with the Black Sea and restoring control of Moscow since it had won over by Russian Tsar against Tatar-Mongols about two hundred years back, even as this has resulted in high cost to Russia with conflict with Ukraine and economic sanctions by the Western countries. As expected majority of Russians have appreciated and supported annexation of Crimea.

It is important to note that agitations in several parts of Russia over issues concerning political freedom and human rights and arrest of hundreds of agitating young Russians during the last few years led by Alexei Navalny who has challenged Putin's leadership. It may be argued that Putin has taken these decisions in the interest of Russia even as few issues have affected his popularity rating.

Economic Scenario

Russia having passed through economic crisis as a result of the breakup of the Soviet Union during the decade of 1990's under Yeltsin's presidency faced sharp decline in GDP growth rate and foreign trade, high inflation, rising unemployment etc. Russia did experience high economic growth during the period 2000-2007 as a result of rising international price for oil and increase in Russia's exports of oil bringing billions of petrodollars. But the country experienced financial crisis due to decline in oil prices since 2008 and rising inflation rate as high as 12-15 percent. GDP growth rate has declined to just about three percent during 2018 and 2019.

Putin has reason to be happy since even as domestic economy has been facing formidable challenges, Russia's foreign trade has significantly increased during his leadership. More importantly Russia continues to be a net exporter with overall exports rising from about $ 100 billion in 2000 to about $ 500 billion in 2018 while imports rose from about $ 60 to $ 300 in respective years. Minerals and metal are major items of foreign trade. Endowed with huge hydrocarbon resources, Russia has been a major exporter of oil and natural gas both to Germany and few European countries as well as to China thus emerging as Energy Superpower. Equally significant is the fact that Russia continues to be a major exporter of military and defence equipments to Middle East countries, China and India.

Putin's popularity rate was increasing during 2004 to 2008 with rising income of Russians when Russian economy was flourishing due to increase in oil exports and rise in international prices from less than 50 dollars in 2004 to about 145 dollars per barrel in 2007 resulting in huge inflow of petrodollars. But decline in oil prices during the last few years have affected Russian economy, thus exposing Russia's overdependence of energy exports.

Putin can also take credit for boosting Russian economic strength as it is evident from the fact that total value of hard currency reserves and gold have increased from $27 billion in 2000 to $ 460 billion in 2018. Thus, Russia has emerged as the fifth-largest state having hard currency and gold reserves in the world. However, this is not reflecting on the strength of economy as exchange rate of Ruble against dollar has declined significantly from about 30 Rubles in 2000 to over 60 Rubles in 2018.

Defence sector continues to get high priority for Putin as Russia's defence expenditure accounts for four percent of GDP in 2018 which in percentage terms more than that of USA or China. But in real terms it is 10 times less than that of USA. However, Putin has claimed that Russia has focused on modernisation of defence equipments which might be contested by some critics.

Demograpic Paralysis

Russia has been facing critical demographic problem as total population has declined from 146 million in 2000 to 143 million in 2008 marginally rising to 145 million in 2019. As per CIA estimates death rate is higher than birth rate and average life expectancy has declined from over 72 years during the Soviet era to below 60 years at present due to lack of priority to health sector and high cost of medicines. About 35-40 percent of population have below average income, it should be a matter of great concern for Putin that Russia's average life expectancy is still several years lower than the average than that in European countries according to European Union statistics released in 2019.

To overcome the problem of demographic decline, in 2007 Putin during his second term of presidency initiated "maternal capital" payments system as a way of bolstering Russia's sagging birth rate. Putin ordered an increase in payments aimed at encouraging Russians to have more children and has signed into law the second welfare initiative to usher in 2020. Moreover, Putin has declared increase in monthly payments to families who have a second child by 3.8 percent compared with 2017: to 466,000 rubles ($7,510). This is because in a report released on 27th December 2019, the State Statistics Service lowered its projection for the next 16 years, with a worst-case scenario showing that the country's population could drop by more than 12 million by 2036. The United Nations has predicted that Russia might lose up to 15 percent of its population by 2050 reaching to 125 million.

External Ties

On external front, Putin has managed to deal with problems to a great extent. Confronted with adversities and economic sanctions by the Western powers, even as he has tried to keep his cordial personal relations with few leaders including the US president Trump and German president Merkel, Putin has succeeded to shift the focus from West to East strengthening ties with China and few Middle East countries. Relations with India have been close and cordial.

Coming to near abroad, being unhappy with the breakup of the former Soviet Union, about which Putin has frankly expressed his view, it is a matter of great significance that Putin has keen interest to form political 'Re-Union' with Belarus and Ukraine which have Slavic identity and geographical contiguity and close economic ties even during the Soviet era. Even as Putin's vision and aim are understandable, reality has been highly complex. Russia is energy rich and oil exporter while Belarus and Ukraine are energy deficit hence energy importers. Hence Putin has even used energy as a weapon by offering to supply oil and natural gas at concessional rate if they become part of 'Re-Union'. This may not be realistic due to on-going conflict with Ukraine particularly since 2014 after annexation of Crimea. But Putin has not given up hopes to pursue his vision with Belarus. Of late Russian President Vladimir Putin and Belarusian President Alyaksandr Lukashenka have held several meetings in 2019 to discuss the Union proeess. As opined by analysts Russia has been using the threat of high energy prices as leverage to pressure Belarus to complete a 20-year-old agreement to form a Union State. On 31st December 2019 Russia and Belarus have reached an agreement on gas prices and amount of gas shipped at the level of 2019 as Kremlin hopes for the integration of the two countries.

But Lukashenka, who has been in power for 25 years, has sought to maintain his nation's independence and even making overtones to the West. There are also political parties, social groups and many young citizens in Belarus want to retain their independence and not to become part of Union with Russia. Recently even official of Belarus's Defense Ministry stated that it was in talks about holding peacekeeping exercises with forces from NATO-member Italy. Hence it is a challenge for Putin to make his vision of forming 'Re-Union' a reality.

In lieu of conclusion it may be stated that as visualised by Boris Yeltsin, Putin has emerged as a powerful, authoritarian leader of Russia during the last 20 years. Despite problems and challenges persisting in the country and growing discontentment and displeasure among some sections of Russian population, Vladimir Putin might continue his leadership of Russia for some more time.

6

Putin's Bombshell "Real Change for Russia"?

Russian President Vladimir Putin's address to the Duma and decisions taken in the third week of January 2020 announcing the need for the constitutional reforms and the resignations of Prime Minister Dmitry Medvedev and the Russian Government were a thunderbolt in the clear sky for Russia. It could be argued that while there is relative political stability in Russia under the partnership of Putin and Medvedev during the last nearly two decades and hence this is a bombshell. Moreover, Putin proposed less known 53-year old career bureaucrat, tax chief Mikhail Mishustin as the new Prime Minister which was approved by the Lower House of State Duma and the new government was formed.

Several questions arise as to what are the reasons for these decisions, what are Putin's objectives and personal interests since he has total control of power over Russia for over 20 years? An effort has been made to examine some of these issues.

Firstly, in the opinion of many Russian analysts, reorganisation of the Russian Government and bringing in new experts and leaders could be in the mind of Putin to solve many socio-economic problems persisting in the country. Mention may be made of the declining trend in economic growth, rising inflation, growing unemployment, decline in per capita income, decline in population, worsening conditions affecting older generation— all leading to increase in social unrest. There were protests going on in the country during the last couple of years against the worsening situation in Russia.

Secondly, Putin is aware of the fact that particularly younger generation want more freedom apart from better economic conditions in the country and are demanding 'Change' leading to violent protests during the last few years. In fact, some of the protests were against the leadership of Putin himself, which he is certainly aware of. Hence sensing the mood of the people Putin seems to have taken this decision to bring about 'Changes'. In fact, the new Prime Minister Mishustin has promised 'Real Changes'. Mishustin has long experience in handling financial matters being at the helm of Russia's tax service which may help in solving many economic problems facing the country. For instance, Mishustin said his priority would be to increase citizens' real income, restoring trust with the business community and drive innovation.

Thirdly, Putin has stated that as a part of the 'Change', the Russian Constitution will be amended giving more authority to Parliament transferring from the President. The State Duma, the Lower House of Parliament, will have the right to name Cabinet Ministers and the Prime Minister, a power that currently belongs to the President. This implies Putin's constitutional reform would 'Change' the balance of power. In other words once the reform process is implemented, the future President will be less powerful than what Putin had enjoyed.

In fact, several top Russian officials who are proxies for Kremlin thinking have been discussing possible changes to the Constitution in the last couple of years. Putin has decided to make 'Changes' in the Constitution since it will be difficult if United Russia party, which is not retaining its popularity, will not be able to regain majority in the State Duma in 2021.

Fourthly, Putin has taken this decision for major 'Changes' in the government and Constitution not without consulting Medvedev. This is evident from the fact that Medvedev stated: "After the [constitutional] changes are adopted, and most likely this will be done after discussions/there will be significant changes...in the balance of power," In announcing the government resignation, Putin said that Medvedev would move over to the National Security Council, to become the Deputy Chairman.

The Security Council itself is a powerful consultative body, whose membership includes the chief of the country's most powerful security agencies: the Federal Security Service, the Foreign Intelligence Service, the Foreign, Defence, and Internal Affairs Ministries; and the head of the National Guard.

It is opined by Aleksei Venediktov, the editor-in-chief of Ekho Moskvy radio and a veteran watcher of Kremlin politics, that for Medvedev who has not earned great popularity during the last over a decade, shifting from the prime ministerial position to Deputy Chairman, would be a promotion. Moreover, he will continue to be close to Putin in a wide spectrum of political, economic and security-related policy-making decisions.

Fifthly, Putin has realised that due to policies pursued by him during the last over a decade, Russia has shifted toward the autarky system, virtual isolation resulting in necessity not to depend much on external trade or assistance as opined by Russia's, political analyst, Dmitry Oreshkin. This has adversely impacted on the Russian economy which is already facing a declining trend, necessitating focus on internal capabilities.

Sixthly, Putin's decision of annexation of Crimea in 2014, even though supported by Russians and giving him high popularity rating, resulted in condemnation and economic sanctions and isolation of Russia by Western countries and geopolitical solitude. Economic sanctions have resulted in major Russian banks being blocked from accessing foreign credit markets hurting external trade. It is a matter of great significance that Russia has been facing adverse criticism and losing cases in the International Court of Justice and European Court of Human Rights.

Lastly, there is a strong possibility that Putin, by giving up his position as President, could take up the position as Chief of State Council, where his long-time partner Medvedev will be the Deputy Chief, and wield authority and decision-making powers in Russia's domestic and foreign policy affairs, giving up day-to-day handling of issues. According to Tatyana Stanovaya, a longtime analyst of Kremlin politics, Putin might be angling to move into the position of head of the State Council after he leaves the presidency. Yevgeny Roizman, former Yekaterinburg mayor and Opposition politician, has commented: “It seems that some configuration [of government] will probably change. All the actions that are taking place now are actions aimed at keeping Putin in power indefinitely.” In support of this contention Aleksei Navalny, Russia’s most prominent Opposition leader and Kremlin critic, has made a candid remark that Putin wants himself and his regime to retain power after his term ends in 2024.

Thus, by declaring most unexpected decisions for ‘Change’, Vladimir Putin being a powerful and shrewd political leader, has shaken social, political and economic institutions in the country for promoting national interest. At the same time he has created opportunities for himself to retain his authority and leadership of Russia in the ‘Changing Scenario’.

Mainstream, VOL LVIII No 30, New Delhi, July 11, 2020

Russia’s Amendments to The Constitution-Official Version Vs Opposition Response

On 3rd July 2020 Russian President Vladimir Putin signed a decree that will bring into force a sweeping package of constitutional amendments that were approved overwhelmingly by Russians. According to Russia’s Central Election Commission, 65 pc of voters participated in the week long voting from 25th June to 1st July 2020 with 78 pc ballots approving the package of more than 200 amendments to the Russian Constitution. This is a significant political development in contemporary Russia and hence an effort has been made to highlight official version of amendment as also domestic opposition response since these amendments have also raised controversy and criticism both in Russia and in the West.

Official Version

Firstly, as per official version, few basic contents of the amendment are — they broaden the powers of the parliament in the formation of the government and redistribute some authority among various government structures, enable Putin to seek additional terms as president since under the current rules the president is forbidden from seeking a third consecutive six-year term. Moreover, amendments also explicitly state the priority of Russian law over international law, ban same-sex marriages, describe a "belief in God" as a core national value, define the Russian language as "the language of the state-forming ethnicity," and make it "impossible to alienate parts of the Russian Federation." The last amendment has great relevance considering the history of the breakup of the former Soviet Union since such provision was not there in the past. In the 1993 constitution it was mentioned that Russia is a secular state.

Secondly, on the 11th March 2020 the package of more than 200 amendments, which were discussed the previous day, were adopted by both lower house of parliament namely the State Duma and the upper chamber, the Federation Council adopting due process to put forth for voting.

Thirdly, Putin has asserted that the proposed constitutional changes would help "reinforce" Russia's traditional "values and principles." Moreover, according to official sources the amendments are necessary for the country's stability and security considering the fact that Russia is the largest country in the world with diverse ethnic communities speaking different languages. Hence some parts of the amendment have great relevance since during the last over two decades Russia has passed through conflict of interests by some regional groups for the breakup of Russia.

Fourthly, as expected percentage of voting varied from place to place - 66 pc in Moscow and 62 pc in St. Petersburg. In few areas such as Chechnya, Siberian region of Tyva 97 pc of voters were in favor of amendments. In contrast to that Nenets Autonomous Okrug, Yakutia, Kamchatka in the Far Eastern region of Russia are some of the regions where a large section of people voted against amendment to the constitution, which was unofficially brushed off by the Kremlin as reported by Interfax news agency. It is surprising that there was no minimum turnout required to make the process of voting valid and voters were given the option of accepting or rejecting the entire package of amendments. Hence as rightly opined by some analysts, the result was seen by many as a foregone conclusion and copies of the new constitution were already on sale in bookshops weeks ahead of the ballot. Dmitry Peskov spokesperson of Kremlin and State Duma speaker Vyacheslav Volodin have stated that high turnout and high level of support to an amendment to the constitution was an indication of Putin's popularity.

Fifth, it is important to note that Central Election Commission head Ella Pamfilova told Interfax on 2nd July that balloting had been transparent and that officials had done everything to ensure its integrity and hence the results "speak to the accuracy of the vote count." By calling it 'nationwide vote' there was no stringent requirement of minimum turnout to make it legal.

Opposition Response

There is considerable criticism to this amendment of the Constitution by the opposition and analysts. Firstly, as expected some sections of opposition leaders have not supported the amendment. For instance, the Communist Party of Russia had called for a "no" vote campaign, the Yabloko party called for a boycott of the plebiscite and others including prominent opposition leader Alexei Navalny said he would "never recognize this result". Some opposition leaders have alleged that high turnout and support reflected in official results were engineered to confirm with targets set down well in advance by the government. As reported by some media reports, on 10th March the wording that would allow Vladimir Putin to seek reelection in 2024 and 2030 was abruptly added when Duma was to give consent for amendments of the Constitution, by which it might be contended that this was done under pressure.

Secondly, Putin's critics charge and insist that the Constitutional amendments are a bid for the 67-year-old Putin to secure power beyond 2024 when his present term will be over. There were several protest marches by activists in Red Square in Moscow and in a few cities before and during the week of voting. But not caring for the protests to show his strength and determination, Vladimir Putin after casting his vote in Moscow stated that he might take part in 2024 presidential election.

Thirdly, sweeping constitutional reforms have sparked sharp criticism from opposition members and human rights groups. There are critics who contend that Putin has weakened democratic institutions, marginalized political opponents and stifled criticism. According to Levada Center polling agency Putin's popularity rate has sank to 59 percent as voting was taking place amid growing discontent in Russia. As opined by Irina Borogan, an investigative journalist "After the vote for the Constitution amendments Russia became China politically, and we lost all the legacy of the new democracy that had emerged in 1991." Notwithstanding that Putin's supporters give him credit for strengthening the country and its economy after the breakup of the former Soviet Union and the crises in the 1990s and make remerge as a major power.

Fourthly, contrary to the contention of the Election Commission, there were reports of irregularities at some polling stations such as double voting, violation of secrecy and intimidation of activists and journalists seeking to monitor the vote. It was reported that two police officers broke a journalist's arm at a polling station on 30th June in St. Petersburg who was on his duty for independent outlet Mediazona which has hit media headlines.

In fact there were different types of irregularities and as reported by Russia analyst from Europe Matthew Luxmoore on 28th June, a Russian woman living in Israel reported that she had been able to vote three times, in Tel Aviv, in Haifa, and again online. At one Moscow polling station, when a man came for casting his vote, he was told that he and his entire family had already cast their votes despite none of them had. In view of all such information, the European Union has called on Russia to probe reports of irregularities.

Fifthly, the EU has also criticized an amendment of the reform that gave Russian law primacy over its international commitments, which defied the decisions of the European Court of Human Rights, of which Moscow is a signatory. The EU spokesman Stano has made a candid statement "We expect Russia, regardless of any amendments to this constitution, to live up to its international obligations". Equally important is the fact that ethnic minorities have expressed concern that the new constitutional wording granting the Russian language special status will lead to the further marginalization of indigenous tongues.

Sixth, the issue arises as to what was the need for amendment to the constitution. In this regard in the past on more than one occasion Putin himself had stated that he will not change the Constitution adopted in 1993. In fact Moscow-based political scientist Yekaterina Schulmann has recalled that Putin, who as recently as 2018 proudly emphasized that he had never altered the constitution. But on 15th Jan 2020 Putin made an announcement about proposed constitutional changes in a state-of-the-nation speech.

Seventh, as per the present Constitution, Putin who has been in power as president for two terms cannot contest election in 2024. But one amendment to the Constitution resets Putin's term-limit clock to zero opening the way for him to run for presidency for reelection when his current six-year term expires in 2024 and that he can contest in 2030 to remain in power till 2036. In view of this William Pomeranz, who is an expert on Russian law and deputy director of the Kennan Institute at the Wilson Center in Washington has opined "The retention of power, as opposed to any far-off historical legacy, appears to be the driving force."

In lieu of conclusion it may be stated that considering the fact that Russia has been passing through several domestic, regional and global socio-economic and political developments and problems during the last nearly three decades, amendments to the constitution were necessary and desirable. The Russian president Vladimir Putin with his vision and valor has enabled Russia to remain secure and stable and re-emerge as a major power in the world. Hence even as some aspects of criticism raised by the EU are relevant, over emphasis by opposition leaders only one element of the amendment to the constitution may not be justifiable.

DR R.G.Gidadhbli is Professor and Former Director, Center for Central Eurasian Studies, University of Mumbai, Mumbai

Section II - Russia in Global Affairs

7

Russia-China Relations—Role of Far East

On July 1, 2005 the President of Russia, Vladimir Putin, and the President of China, Hu Jintao, signed several documents during the latter's Visit to Moscow. The summit meeting between the two leaders and agreements reached during the summit are expected to reinforce the relations between Russia and China. In fact, there has been a qualitative improvement in the political relations between Russia and China during the last decade and the two countries have established a strategic partnership. Russia has been the largest source of defence related equipments to China including hi-tech machinery and in August 2005 both the countries have also undertaken joint military exercises. In the economic sphere, from a negligible quantity of trade before the Soviet breakup, China has emerged as a major trading partner of Russia at present when the total trade turnover between the two countries has amounted to about $ 20 billion.

A communique released subsequent to the summit affirmed the goal of 'strategic cooperation' between Russia and China and the 'Russian-Chinese Action Plan for 2005-2008'. As reported by the Interfax, the two leaders also signed a Joint Declaration 'On the International Order in the Twenty-first Century'. The essence of this important declaration lies in the fact that both Russia and China are in favour of a multi-polar world and they do not want the superpower hegemony of the USA in world affairs. Specifically, both

Vladimir Putin and Hu Jintao seem to be against the idea of imposing a Western socio-political model of development for the countries in transition. This is understandable because Russia has come under considerable criticism from the West on various policy measures initiated by Putin with regard to centralisation of powers, curbing the role of political parties, undermining the independence of the judiciary, matters relating to human rights and ethnic minorities and so on. Moreover, Putin might also have legitimate concern about the growing US influence on Georgia and Ukraine, which have witnessed recently velvet and orange revolutions in which there was speculation of indirect support by the USA. Hence Putin might be worried about the likely spillover effects of these developments on Russia itself and on other member-nations of the Commonwealth of Independent States. Similarly, Chinese leaders have their own concerns, since the country has retained the communist political system with single-party rule and the leadership does not want it to be disturbed. Apart from these factors, Russia and China, being members of the Shanghai Cooperation Organisation, are also concerned about the increasing role of the USA in the Central Asian region. In this regard, an important observation has been made by Konstantin Pulikovskii, who is the Presidential envoy to the Far East, when he stated that closer relationship with China is a geopolitical objective linked with the strengthening of Russia's position in the world.

It is pertinent to note that Russia's Far Eastern regions and East Siberia have an important role in the Russia-China relations. This is evident from the fact that after the summit meeting with Vladimir Putin, the Chinese President met the Governors of East Siberia and the Far Eastern regions on his way-back to China. While socio-political and economic relations between the Far Eastern regions and China are expected to increase in the years to come, it may be worthwhile to examine the role of the Far East in Russia-China relations during the last over a decade. This is particularly important because on certain issues there were differences in the views and perceptions among the policy-makers and academic community in Russia and China. There are three aspects which assume significance in examining the role of the Far East in Russia's relations with China— the common border with China, the influx of the Chinese and economic relations.

Russia-China Border Issue

It is significant to note that the latest summit meeting between the Presidents of Russia and China has taken place when the two countries have amicably resolved the border dispute. On the Far Eastern parts of the country, Russia has over 4300 km long border with China. So far the unsettled border issue had been a major irritant in the relations between the two countries. The former Soviet Union and China had military conflicts on the Ussuri sector in the 1960s. In fact, this problem is a hangover of the historical past. According to specialists, the 1860 Russian-Chinese border treaty had not carried out the delimitation in the case of Amur and Ussuri water areas.

Even the 1991 agreement between Russia and China could not clear the ambiguity. At last in October 2004, Putin and Hu could finally resolve the border dispute by entering into an agreement, which has been ratified by the respective governments and legislative bodies. In essence the agreement delimited the eastern border into two sections—(a) near the Bolshoi island in the upper reaches of the Argun river (Chita region) and (b) near the islands Tabarovsk and Bolshoi Ussuriski near the city of Khabarovsk. Hence the Chinese President has rightly stated that with the resolution of the border dispute, Russia-China relations have entered 'a new historic epoch'.

The significance of the agreement on the boundary issue lies in the fact that Vladimir Putin has been able to resolve the conflicts of interest that prevailed within Russia between the central leadership and regional leaders during the last decade. For instance, in the 1990s the Governor of Khabarovsk Krai, Viktor Ishaev, had strong differences with the central leadership on the issue of demarcation of the Russia-China boundary. Similarly the chief of Primorsk Krai also stated in 1995 that regional heads were fighting against the demarcation of boundary with the leaders in Moscow. This shows that there were apprehensions in the minds of some regional leaders on the boundary issue and about the relations with China, which were partly rooted in history. In May 1994, Ishaev stated: "We are feeling hidden expansion of China in Russia's Far East which will degrade Russia." Presumably for this reason he declared that not a single square inch of land will be given to China. Hence before the agreement was signed in October 2004 there was resistance by regional leaders against giving away the Tabarovsk island and a part of the island on Great Ussuri river to China. There were heated arguments in the Duma when the proposed agreement was placed for legislative approval.

But after Putin signed the border agreement with China in October 2004, there has been a major change in the statements and perceptions of leaders from the Far Eastern region on this issue. Hence some Russian and Chinese scholars have opined that while under Boris Yeltsin the regional leaders were assertive, the views of the strong central leadership of Putin has prevailed over the views of regional leaders. This is partly because Putin as the President has managed to acquire enormous powers to appoint and dismiss Governors and hence unlike in the past they are not assertive and belligerent in challenging the views of the central leadership. Thus, a Chinese scholar has opined that regional leaders are not able to use the 'Chinese threat card' after the Russia-China border agreement has been made. It also appears that many regional heads are in agreement with Putin who has visualised a larger role for Russia in world affairs which will benefit these regions as well and hence Putin's resolve to solve the border dispute with China has been welcomed by some of them.

Perception of Chinese Expansion in the Far East

The perception among Russians about the Chinese expansion in the Far East has played an important role in Russia-China relations. This perception may be attributed to two factors—the presence of a large number of Chinese in Russia's Far East and the nature of their activities in these regions. For some time this has adversely affected the relations between the two countries. To put the issue in the proper perspective it may be stated that in 1988 the Chinese were permitted to enter the Soviet Union without visa as workers and traders. After the Soviet breakup in 1992 Russia and China entered into an agreement for the exchange of citizens without visa. On this issue some Russian leaders have opined that in the early 1990s this policy has resulted in a massive influx of the Chinese into the Far East. According to Russian specialists, in 1992 the number of Chinese entering Russia's Far East was over 200,000, which was more than four times than that in the previous year.

In 1993 alone over 150,000 Chinese citizens entered the Primorsk Krai. In some sections of the Russian press there were articles about the threat of 'Chinese expansion' and 'Yellow Danger' quoting the entry of up to two million Chinese during 1992-93 into the Far Eastern regions. Viktor Larin has quoted a Russian astrologer who predicted that by 2040 the Primorsk Krai will be Chinese and cease to be Russian. Hence there was growing concern among the elite and even among common Russians that they may not feel masters in their own land. The influx of the Chinese and threat perception of 'Chinese expansion' into Russia's Far East seem to have affected the views of ordinary Russian citizens on Russia-China relations. According to L. Larina, in a survey conducted in 1994 only one-third of respondents expressed 'good' opinion towards relations with China, while 38 percent were 'indifferent' and 23 percent felt 'bad'. In her opinion the survey conducted in 2003 did not show any major change in the views.

Apart from the sheer number of immigrants, there were allegations about a large number of Chinese staying and working illegally and some of them carrying out illegal and criminal activities. In 1993, some Russian specialists reported that about 400,000 Chinese were staying and working illegally in the Far Eastern regions. This problem seems to have caused concern to the local authorities. However, it appears that during 1994-98 measures were taken by the local Russian governments against illegal migrants from China and their illegal activities.

However, on the question of the number of Chinese in Russia's Far East, Chinese scholar Inn Tszanpin has contended that the contentions of Russian specialists were highly exaggerated. To substantiate his view he has quoted the estimates of the Cameigi Foundation report of 1996 according to which there were between 200,000 to-300,000 Chinese living between the Lake Baikal region and Primorsk Krai. This number is much less than the estimates of Russian scholars. Moreover, Inn Tszanpin has pointed out that the number of Chinese workers permanently settled in the Far Fast was not more than 150-200 thousand. On this basis he has discounted the allegation of 'Chinese threat' or 'Chinese expansion' in the Far Eastern regions of Russia. ('View Outside Limit of Old Problems: Experience of Russia-Chinese Border Cooperation', Occasional Paper No. 6, June 2005, Slavic Research Centre.' Hokkaido University, Sapporo, Japan)

Notwithstanding these differences in the estimates and perceptions about the presence of the Chinese labour force in Russia's Far East, the fact remains that the influx of Chinese into the Far East has been caused by the disproportion in the number of population on either side of the border. As against only seven million on the Russian side of the border, there are over 120 million people living on the Chinese side of the border. Hence there has been demographic pressure on the Chinese side and a natural tendency to migrate to the neighbouring regions of Russia when the entry became easier. During the last few years Putin seems to have taken effective measures along with the Chinese Government with regard to illegal migration from the Chinese side. However, according to some specialists, every year about 20,000 Chinese workers enter Russia's Far East.

While there has been no consensus about the number of illegal Chinese inhabitants in Russia, Chinese specialists have highlighted several shortcomings in Russia's policy on immigration. Firstly, it is observed that the quota decided by the Russian Government for giving visas to the immigrant workers was reported to be far less than the demand for labour force in the Far East. For instance, in 2004 while the Primorski Krai needed about 70,000 workers, the quota for migrants was only 15,000. Hence illegal methods were used for meeting the growing demand for labour. Thus, Chinese specialists feel that that the quota system needed to be revised. Secondly, some specialists have opined that the Russian Government has fixed heavy charges when legal procedures and formalities are to be followed for inviting foreign labour. As pointed out by a Chinese specialist, the cost was about 3000 roubles per worker, plus visa charges, and other related expenses. The Chinese firm, which recruits and makes arrangement for labour for its Russian employer, also charges some money. But in contrast to this when a Russian employer hires workers illegally he has to pay penalty amount, which is comparatively much less. Hence the Russian policy has inadvertently contributed to large-scale illegal migration of Chinese workers into the Far East. There is a paradoxical situation, which needed to be rectified since the local governments have been losing revenue. Thirdly, it appears that there is high level of corruption on both sides of the border, which might also be contributing to this situation.

Notwithstanding these differences in estimates and interpretations there is a general consensus among the Russian specialists and bureaucrats that during the last 10-15 years Chinese workers have contributed significantly to the economic development of the Far East. While Russia's Far East has rich resource potentialities in terms of energy resources, minerals, chemicals, forest and large cultivable agricultural land, there has been great shortage of labour force to exploit these resources. Since Russia's population growth has declined during the last few decades, the Far East regions have to depend upon outside labour. In fact, as observed by O. Maltsev, without the labour force from China, Russia will find it difficult to develop the Far East and exploit the region's natural resources.

Economic Relations

The Eastern parts of Siberia and the Far Eastern regions have an important role to play in Russia-China economic relations and their role is expected to increase significantly in the future. The importance of the Far East in Russia-China economic relations is in sharp contrast to its insignificant role during the last three decades of the Soviet era. This is mainly because in the past, major decisions on matters relating to Soviet foreign trade were taken in Moscow. Hence the Far Eastern regions had hardly any role to play. But after the Soviet break-up, the leaders of the Far Eastern regions were able to take the initiative in trading with the neighbouring areas of China. However, initially the quantum of trade was not much. But since Putin came to power as the President there has been improvement in the share of the Far East in Russia-China trade. According to some Chinese specialists, the 'China Threat' had been transformed into 'working factor' in the economic development of Russia's Far East. This is because several steps have been taken in this regard.

In June 2004, the Khabarovsk Krai Govrernment along with the Ministry of Trade of the Russian Government set up the first Russia-China Investment Forum in Khabarovsk in which over 500 Russian and Chinese businessmen participated. Secondly, considerable attention has been paid for large scale infrastructure development, including modernising the road network in the Far East with China. Thirdly, the concept of 'Single Economic Space' has been evolved comprising Russia's Far Eastern oblasts, Siberian territory and China's Central-South provinces. This has helped stable growth of trade between the two countries. Fourthly, in order to attract greater Chinese involvement in the economic development of the Far East, the Russian Government had adopted an auction system with the right to develop natural resources of the Far East. It is a fact that many Chinese businessmen have won timber concessions as they were more efficient than domestic businessmen. Russia's Minister of Economy, German Gref, stated at the Russia-China Investment Forum in Khabarovsk in 2004 that Russia might adopt laws to create 'Special Economic Zones' in various parts of Russia including in the Far East. The Russian Government hopes to attract foreign capital in these zones because many facilities will be provided to foreign firms including 99 years lease of territory. This may create new possibilities for the Chinese for investment and also getting labour on a long-term basis.

All these developments seem to have helped significantly to increase the Chinese trade with the Far East regions. From an insignificant volume of trade in 1992 in 2002 the share of border regions (Khabarovsk, Amur, Chita etc.) was about $ 1.5 billion, that is, 12 percent in Russia-China trade. The percentage share of imports in these regions from China has increased from about 40 in 1997 to about 80 in 2002 although the percentage varies for different oblasts. Hence some Russian economists argue that these border regions have become totally dependent upon China for a wide range of consumer goods— fruits, vegetables, garments, knitted wear, footwear etc. which is not in Russia's interest. Efforts have been made to diversify to enhance trade with South Korea, Japan, Vietnam and so on. On this issue the Chinese scholars' argument is that imports from China were necessary since the Far Eastern regions were not able to meet the needs of the population.

On some of the issues of economic relations between the two countries, there are differences in viewpoints among specialists in Russia and China with regard to the trade relations between the two countries. Firstly, in the opinion of some Russian economists large-scale imports from China has affected the development of domestic industries of many Far Eastern oblasts. There were reports that during the last decade many industrial units producing consumer goods were closed down. According to Russian academic Viktor Larin, this was mainly because Chinese goods were cheaper by 50-80 percent by virtue of disparity in the cost of production. It is pointed out by Nina Pashkova that the Chinese Government had been giving heavy subsidy and tax concessions making Chinese goods cheaper besides low wages in China as compared to those in Russia. But disagreeing with this view, Chinese specialist Inn Tszanpin has stated that in 2002 China had a trade deficit with Russia to the tune of over $ 3 billion and hence the Chinese Government stimulated exports to Russia. Secondly, despite the large volume of trade, China had not invested much in the economic development of the Far East. For instance, in 2003 China's investment was negligible in the Far East, a mere $ 13.4 million out of the total foreign direct investment of over $ 2.9 billion, that is, about 0.47 percent of the total investment. In Amur oblast the Chinese share was about 11 percent of the total foreign investment. While the local governments in the Russian Far East legitimately expected greater investment from China, the Chinese businessmen seem to have felt that the ownership rights and other conditions for investment opportunities were not sufficiently attractive. Thirdly, it was pointed out by Russian economists that there was large-scale 'grey' criminal business carried out by the Chinese in the border regions of the Far East. Substantial quantities of goods were being brought into Russia without paying import duties and other taxes and dumping goods in the Russian market. Moreover, there were also reports about contraband goods brought into the border cities and regions. Fourthly, according to Russian specialists, firms and traders from Russia suffered from weak information about their Chinese partners. There was also absence of control over the quality of goods being brought into Russia from China. Moreover, it appears that, according to Russian traders, there was lack of mechanism in China for solving economic disputes with the Chinese partners. These differences may be resolved after the latest summit meeting between the Presidents of the two countries. In fact, there are good prospects of increasing trade and economic relations in the future. Energy resources of Siberia and the Far East have great potentiality to enhance

Russia-China economic relations in the future. It has been reported that Russia has committed to supply larger quantity of oil-gas to China and thus meeting the 'energy security' needs of China to a great extent. It appears that the first stage of a new strategic pipeline in the Far East will be ready by 2008, which will be terminated at Skovorodina in Amur oblast near the Chinese border with a thorough put capacity of 30 million tons, which might eventually increase to 50 million tons. With such significant increases in imports of oil and gas from Russia, China will be able to reduce its imports from the Middle East countries in the future.

The leaders of Russia and China have finalised a perspective plan for promoting trade between the two countries according to which Russia's total trade turnover with China is expected to increase from about $ 20 billion in 2004 to about $ 60-80 billion by 2010. In that scenario trade and economic ties betwen the Far Eastern regions and China will increase significantly. Since 2004 the Chinese leaders and business firms have shown interest in increasing investment in Russia. As reported in the Russian press, China will invest over $ 12-20 billion in the Russian economy in the next five to seven years, which includes investment in projects in the Far East. Putin has stated in 2004 that the GDP of Russia should be doubled by 2010. While this seems to be rather ambitious, he might expect that the Far Eastern regions will also contribute in this regard with their enhanced trade and economic relations with China.

In lieu of conclusion it may be stated that through the June 2005 summit, the Presidents of both Russia and China are interested in—securing their respective national interests, enhancing their role in the world affairs, and containing the growing influence of the USA in their own spheres of influence. Valdimir Putin and Hu Jintao have resolved their historical border dispute and few other issues, which are expected to create a new era in Russia-China relations. However, differences in the assessments between Russian and Chinese specialists and in the perceptions among some sections of the Russian population on the Chinese role in Russia's Far East might not have been fully resolved.

8

Re-emergence of Russia: Implications for Southeast Asia

During the last five to six years under the leadership of former president Vladimir Putin, Russia has re-emerged as a major player in international affairs. Russia is now under the presidency of Dmitri Medvedev who was chosen by Putin even as Putin himself had taken charge as prime minister of the country from June 2008. Hence in the context of Russia's relations with the Asia-Pacific region in general and Southeast Asia in particular, it may be worthwhile to enquire into the following:

> What are the factors that have contributed to the re-emergence of Russia? What is the state of relations between Russia and the West and what are their implications for Southeast Asian countries? What are Russia's key interests and priorities in Southeast Asia and what are the likely priorities of Russia under the new team of Medvedev and Putin?

A variety of factors seem to have contributed to the re-emergence of Russia. Firstly, unlike the crisis conditions that prevailed in Russia in the aftermath of the Soviet break-up of the 1990s, in the eight years under the Putin presidency, the country has attained substantial

---

This publication is based on the papers the writers presented at the 22nd Asia Pacific Roundtable, Kuala Lumpur, Malaysia, 4-8 June 2008.

political strength and stability. Specifically during the second term of Putin's presidency that ended by the middle of 2008, Russia followed several policy measures which have led to:

(a) Centralisation of political power, which has effectively enhanced the powers of the president, and
(b) The weakening of the role of the political parties, including the Communist party, which had offered strong opposition to former president Boris Yeltsin.

Hence, with the concentration of power with the Kremlin, Putin was able to pursue an assertive policy, both in the domestic sphere and in Russia's foreign policy issues. Some western analysts believe that Putin's policies were aggressive in nature and content. But Russian analysts have argued that Putin pursued an assertive foreign policy to serve Russia's national interest. At any rate, policies pursued by Putin increased his popularity at home as a strong leader.

This is also reflected in Russia's 'Near Abroad' policy in which Russia has close relations with the some states, such as the Central Asian States, Belarus, and Armenia, with which there is no conflict of interest. But with a few other states such as Georgia, Ukraine etc. Russia has occasional differences on specific issues, and relations are not always cordial. The Georgia-Russia Five Day War in August 2008, over the issue of the independence of Georgia's breakaway republics of South Ossetia and Abkhazia, was the most unexpected event in the contemporary history of the post-Soviet era.

Even as the ultimate implications of the Georgia-Russia war are not clear, Russia's political and economic relations with Georgia have worsened and Russia's relations with its neighbour, Ukraine, have become highly sensitive, considering the on-going differences between them during the last couple of years.

Secondly, Russia has become economically strong. The country has been able to maintain relatively high GDP growth rates during the last few years. It was about eight percent in 2007 according to Russian official sources, breaking all records of the last two decades. The Russian economy is booming and, as believed by some western analysts, Russia is back in the headlines. According to Russian sources, the country has become one among the seven largest economies in the world. Russia had a budget surplus of six percent in 2007, and the state treasury's coffers were full.

According to World Bank reports, Russia's hard currency reserves were US$447 billion at the end of 2007, as compared to a meagre US$37 billion in 2000. This meant a rise of over 12 times in about eight years, even as according to some finance experts, the country is likely to face some economic challenges (Yevsei Gurvich, 2007:1).

With such vast hard currency reserves, the Russian government has been paying off international debts in advance. The ruble has become a strong currency and has appreciated against the dollar. Per capita income has nearly doubled in the last five years, exceeding $900 at present, hence Russians prefer to hold rubles and not dollars. All these achievements have become possible mainly due to huge hard currency earnings through exports of oil and natural gas, and export of defence equipment.

Being one of the major world producers and exporters of oil and natural gas, Russia has benefited immensely from the rising international market price for oil, from less than US$40 per barrel in 2004, to about US$130 per barrel in the middle of 2008, though declining to below US$100 in September 2008.

With this inflow of petro-dollars, Russian policy-makers are able to reassert themselves in domestic economic issues as also in their dealings abroad. The Russian state sector companies and Russian energy giants such as Gazprom and Rosneft have been able to invest in the energy sector so as to acquire assets such as oil fields and pipelines, both at home and abroad. At the same time, under the leadership of Putin, Russia has followed a policy of 'Resource Nationalism, in order to reduce the share of foreign companies, such as British Petroleum, in joint ventures with Russia. Equally important and significant is the fact that Russian companies have increased their shares in companies abroad, including in Armenia, Belarus, Bulgaria, Kazakhstan, Turkmenistan, Uzbekistan, Algeria, Venezuela etc (Gidadhubli, 2007: 2).

Under Vladimir Putin's presidency, the role of Russia's state sector has increased, contrary to the privatisation policy pursued by

Boris Yeltsin in the 1990s. Moreover, the Russian state, energy giants, and the new class of Russian oligarchs have been working in tandem to achieve the objective of making Russia the 'Energy Superpower' of the world. According to some western analysts, Gazprom is often described in media commentary as a lever of Russian foreign policy, which is an indication of commercial considerations in Russia's foreign policy. Russia has also been a major exporter of ferrous and non-ferrous metals to the global market.

Thirdly, Russia under Putin's presidency has emphasised the increasing of the production and export of arms and military equipment, and modernising the defence sector. This is evident from the fact that while Russia's defence expenditure had gone down by 50 percent between 1992-97, it shot up from 95 billion rubles in 2002 to 344 billion rubles in 2003, and this trend has continued. Russian leaders realised the economic benefits of defence exports, because at a time when the rest of the economy was facing constraints of growth, the defence sector emerged as the major source of export earnings.

Hence in 2003, Putin approved the plan for a new military technical policy on rearmament, emphasising R&D of a new generation of weapons systems. Thus, according to Russian defence expert, Vladimir Artykov, the state organisation, Rosoboronexport, became active in selling arms to various countries, including China, India and to Southeast Asian countries (Vladimir Artyakov, 2006: 3). Annually, Asian countries including China, India etc. purchase more than 90 percent of Russia's US$5 billion arms exports. Thus, Russia has re-emerged as a major exporter of arms to a large number of countries, including China, India, and many other countries in Asia, Africa and Latin America.

Fourthly, Russia has been actively associated with, and is working in, several regional organisations, such as the Collective Security Treaty Organisation, Eurasian Economic Community and so on, and with the former Soviet republics, the present Commonwealth of Independent States. Similarly, Russia has been active in regional organisations such as the Shanghai Co-operation Organisation, Apec, and Asean, enabling Russian leaders to promote their policy initiatives collectively to counter the policies of the West.

Russia-West Relations: Growing Conflict of Interests

There have been ups and downs in Russia's relations with the West after the Soviet break-up; a downward phase was witnessed in the last few years (Michael McFaul, 2004: 4). The relations further worsened from August 2008 when the US and many Western countries accused Russian leaders of 'disproportionate' use of force in 'breaking (the) territorial integrity' of Georgia. Prior to that too, there were mutual accusations from time to time, leading to verbal wars between Russia and the West.

For instance, former US vice president Dick Cheney made an allegation that Russia was an undependable country, on the issue of energy supplies to the West, and that Vladimir Putin was an autocratic leader. Russia's first Deputy Prime Minister Sergei Ivanov retorted in July 2007, saying that the West was creating a 'New Berlin Wall.' Russia's Foreign Minister Sergei Lavrov accused the West of adopting virtually a 'New Cold War' policy towards Russia.

Therefore, there are different views and perceptions about Russia's relations with the West. According to one view articulated by the Russian daily paper *Vretnya Novostei,* 'Europe created as many problems for Russia as (the) opportunities it offered.' Russian President Medvedev has reiterated that he would pursue Putin's policies towards the West (RfeRL, 2008: 5).

Russia is unhappy with the eastward expansion of NATO which has been making efforts to draw Ukraine and Georgia into its military alliance. Russian leaders consider this a security threat to their country. Similarly, Russia's relations with the European Union (EU) are often affected even as the EU is Russia's largest partner in trade and economic relations. There is a view that on certain political issues, Germany is more sympathetic towards Russia, hence EU believes Russia is trying to bring about a division among the EU members.

At the same time, Russia's relations with the Baltic States and Poland, which joined the EU after the Soviet break-up, are strained. One of the major issues that has created great resentment in the West has been Russia's agreement with Iran to build a nuclear power plant at Bushehr. Linked to this Iranian issue has been the US decision to set up a 'Missile Defence Shield' in Europe by installing ten anti-missile interceptors in Poland and a radar unit in the Czech Republic. In retaliation Russia has threatened to put anti-missile units in Kaliningrad in the Baltic region, targeting Europe.

President Medvedev has strongly reiterated and supported the policies and measures initiated by Putin on this issue in the last several years. Although Russia's problems with the West may not have a direct bearing on Asian countries, and on Asean in particular, they may have indirect implications, as Russian policy-makers might be more inclined to turn towards the East to promote their own national and global political and economic interests.

Political Relations between Russia and Southeast Asia

Russia has multi-vectored interest in the Asia Pacific — geopolitical, political, economic and so on. Russia's concept of balance of power, which is fundamental to Moscow's view of the world, has been reflected in Russia's Foreign Policy Concept of July 2000, and in subsequent policies and political decisions. It is determined by the geopolitical interests of Russia, as one of the largest Eurasian powers; hence Russia has tried to assert its position against Western powers in the region. This is evident from the objective of Putin, who wanted Russia to re-emerge as a major world power; Russia's position was affected in the 1990s when it faced major problems both at home and abroad (Gidadhubli, 2007: 6)

Secondly, it is important to note that Russian policymakers have recognised the growing global strategic importance of Asia-Pacific and Asean countries. Hence Russia's 'Took East' policy has been intended to promote its national interest (Buszynski Lesszek, 2006: 7) To fulfil its own political objectives, Russia has significantly intensified its foreign policy towards the Asia Pacific, and undertook measures in recent years to get full membership of Apec and Asean. Thus, Russia's key interest is to increase space and place for its role in this region.

Thirdly, Moscow firmly believes in close co-operation with Southeast Asian countries for mutual benefit, and there has been a strong perception among the Russian policy-makers about the reciprocal response of these countries towards Russia. It is also argued that between Russia and Asean countries, there is a commonality of views on maintaining political stability and building a multi-polar world order. Hence Asean-Russia political and security co-operation is expected to strengthen, given the convergence in interest in ensuring a peaceful region to pursue economic development and to combat the menace of terrorism and transnational crimes.

To achieve Russia's foreign policy goals, Vladimir Putin pursued active political diplomacy with these countries, evident from several visits, for eight years from 2000 to May 2008, during his presidency. For instance, Putin's visit to Hanoi in March 2001 was the first official visit to Vietnam by a Russian head of a State in 50 years, and hence it has great historic significance, not only for Russia's relations with Vietnam, but also for the Southeast Asian region as well.

Thus, Russia pursued a positive external policy under Putin, trying to strike a balance between the East and the West. Putin attended the December 2005 Asean Summit in Malaysia, which was seen as further evidence that Moscow preferred closer interaction with Asia, over integration with the West, because of shared values. Hence at the political level, Russia is confident about active bilateral co-operation with the Asia-Pacific and Asean countries and within international associations including the UN, the Asean Regional Forum (ARF) and the Asia-Pacific Economic Co-operation (Apec).

This has helped the partnership become an influential factor in regional politics and is reflected in the emphasis that Russia has placed on the establishment of a mechanism for regional co-operation between the Asean Regional Forum (ARF) and Shanghai Co-operation Organisation (SCO) for tackling issues concerning security and terrorism effectively. The establishment of a mechanism for co-operation between the ARF and the SCO has in practice already proved its effectiveness and relevance in the task of reinforcing security and combating terrorism in Central Asia.

Russia-Asean Economic Relations

Russia's 'Look East' policy is guided by strong economic considerations. Its increased interest in promoting economic ties with the Asean countries is guided by the region's enormous economic potentialities. Asia accounts for about half the world population and about one-fifth of global trade. It is therefore pragmatic on the part of Russia to be a major player in the Asia Pacific and Southeast Asian region. Neo-liberals argue that three elements have transformed Russia into a predominantly regional player in the Asia Pacific.

Firstly, there is change in the character of Russia's Far Eastern regions and their relationship with the wider region of Asia. The second element is a genuine commitment to strengthening relations with major Asian powers including those in the Asia Pacific. The third element is the 'Economic Factor' — the contention being that economic instruments are often more effective than traditional political and military means in projecting influence. Hence Russia has a keen interest in increasing trade and economic ties with countries in this region.

Trade and economic factors have also contributed to Russia's interest in Southeast Asia, rekindled mainly after Putin took over the presidency in 2000. For the economic development of Siberia and the Russian Far East, Russia wants closer integration with Asian countries and regional institutions including the Asean. Analysts believe that Russia gets support from Southeast Asian countries, including Malaysia. Russia's aggregate trade turnover with the Asean region, which was not significant in 2002, has almost doubled in the past six years. But this is only one-third of the potential trade and technological co-operation. This is why, besides trying to increase trade relations, Russia has been looking for new spheres of cooperation with Asean partners. With significant economic growth during the last few years, Russia wants to shift the focus to co-operation in the 'hi-tech' areas and in the services sector.

An important development in this regard is that in December 2005, foreign ministers from Russia and Asean signed an economic and development co-operation agreement, setting out programmes to deepen ties over the coming decade. Russia also signs bilateral agreements with Southeast Asian countries from time to time. Moreover, Vladimir Putin's regular interaction with several leaders from Southeast Asian countries has helped to bolster ties as well as to strengthen trade and economic ties.

For instance, the Asean-Russia Joint Co-operation Committee (ARJCC), consisting of representatives of official bodies and of business and scientific communities, oversees bilateral economic, trade and research-technical co-operation. This Foundation stepped up its efforts in the past few years, when the Asian vector of Russia's foreign policy gained in strength.

Moreover, bilateral co-operation between Russia and Southeast Asian countries has assumed great economic significance. For instance, Russian authorities have bilateral cooperation with Malaysia to promote interaction in the areas of small and medium enterprises, science and technology, energy, minerals, transport, finance, agriculture, technical co-operation, tourism, information and communication technologies (ICT), environment protection and disaster management. Russia has also signed agreements to hold exhibitions from time to time. According to Russian political analysts, 'high-tech' exhibitions held in the recent past in Kuala Lumpur and Bangkok were a success.

Similarly, Russian research laboratories have received contracts from Singapore for doing research and design projects, including in dual-purpose goods. It is important to note that Russia-Malaysia economic ties have covered many important sectors. This is evident from the joint project in which Malaysia is to invest US$25 million, in three years, to produce leokain and bitomycin, antibiotics for the treatment of wounds and burns. Malaysia is also promoting a project by the Russian company Tana aimed at establishing a network of tele-medical video monitoring centres to help patients with grave infectious diseases, such as tuberculosis, AIDS, and malaria.

Russia has other economic issues of interest in the Southeast Asian region besides promoting trade. For instance, according to a Russian think tank, Russia could emulate many of the experiences of Southeast Asian countries — methods of attracting foreign investment; the establishment of special economic zones and free trade zones; support to small and medium-sized businesses; and the creation of a common regional currency, the Asian Currency Unit (ACU). This is because Russian policy-makers are aware that during the last 20 years or so, Singapore has helped countries like China and Indonesia to build Special Economic Zones (SEZ).

In order to learn from this experiment, the Russian and Singapore governments signed a memorandum of understanding on co-operation in establishing SEZs in 2006. Similarly, Russia plans to make use of Singapore's unique experience in attracting foreign investment and in investing substantial funds abroad. This is because Singapore accounts for 39 percent of total investments in Asia, and it has invested over US $60 million in the Russian economy. This is an important aspect for Russian policy-makers to emulate. Singapore, being a country with low investment risks, attracted investments of about US $5.35 billion in 2006.

Russia-Asean Energy Co-operation

For Russia, energy is an important sphere for promoting cooperation with the Asia-Pacific and Asean countries. According to modest forecasts based on projected rates of economic and demographic growth, global energy consumption will increase by 20 percent in 20 years and it will double by the middle of this century. This will increase Russia's role as an energy provider. Russia plans to play an important role in the Asian countries' growing energy market. As stated by Russian Energy Minister Viktor Khristenko, only three percent of Russia's energy exports went to Asia in 2007.

By 2020, Russia proposes to export 30 percent of its energy exports to Asian countries (Izvestiya, 2007: 8). This statement assumes importance considering the fact that Russia is a member of the Asia-Pacific Economic Co-operation (Apec) Organisation and at one of the bloc's recent summits, Moscow's primary focus was on how it could meet Asia's demand for energy to fuel the region's economic development. The Russian energy giant Gazprom has calculated that Russia, which has the world's largest natural gas reserves, will be able to supply some 110 billion cubic metres of gas to Southeast Asian countries by 2020, with the share of liquefied natural gas (LNG) growing considerably.

Russia has signed a memorandum on strategic co-operation with PTT, Thailand's Oil and Gas Corporation. Gazprom has shown keen interest in joining Malaysia's Petronas in the construction of a gas pipeline across Asean, and on gas supply infrastructure in Asean member countries. Recently, Petronas took part in the initial public offering of Russian state-run oil company Rosneft, buying US $1.1 billion worth of its shares, more than British Petroleum's or China CNPC's investment in it. Hence there is close co-operation in the energy sector.

Apart from exporting oil and natural gas, Russia is interested in exporting machinery and equipment for power plants in Southeast Asia. For instance, Russia's Silovye Mashiny, which produces power machines and equipment, is rapidly strengthening its foothold in the region. The demand for its equipment has grown considerably owing to the construction and modernisation of thermal and hydropower plants in Thailand, Vietnam, Laos and Cambodia. Russian energy companies are seeking to co-operate for mutual benefit in the energy related sector, with the Asia-Pacific and Asean countries. For instance, Russian electricity monopoly RAO UES has also been actively looking for partners and investors in Southeast Asian countries. It was in discussions with Malaysia for the financing of new electricity assets in Russia, hoping that Malaysian partners will invest about US $2 billion in the Russian power generation sector.

Nuclear Energy

Russia is one of the leading producers of nuclear energy in the world. It has several years of experience in nuclear power technologies, including in designing and using fast neutron reactors. The average prime cost of electricity produced by Russian nuclear power plants is claimed to be US $0,014 per Kwh. According to Russian scientists, Russia is one of the world's leaders in the production of small nuclear power units, and hence its achievements could also be used in other countries.

It appears that several countries, notably Indonesia, Malaysia, Thailand and Vietnam, have announced their intention to develop nuclear power plants in their respective power sectors. In this context it may be mentioned that Russian experts are modernising the Da Lat Nuclear Research Reactor, and assembling equipment for the Hanoi gamma-ray unit. Nuclear contracts are also being negotiated with other countries. In particular, Indonesia has proposed to acquire a Russian-made floating nuclear power plant, an exclusive product of Russian engineers.

With Russia being interested in regional projects, mutuality of interests between Russia and the Asean countries provides a reliable foundation for the architecture of future relations. But according to some analysts, even as Southeast Asia is an old stomping ground for the Kremlin, Russia has been late in returning to the scene. Many of the countries have close ties with Western countries and also with China. Hence it is not going to be very easy for Russia to succeed in the region in the short term; it might succeed to some extent in the long run.

Russia is also interested in the Southeast Asian region to secure support for its entry into the World Trade Organisation. Hence as argued by some analysts, Russia's intention to increase its engagement with the Southeast Asian countries is no different from its other foreign policy goals. Kremlin authorities have been engaged in negotiations with several countries to enter the World Trade Organisation.

Export of Defence Equipment

It is important to note that Russia has emerged as a major exporter of defence equipment to many Asean countries, including Vietnam, Malaysia, Indonesia, and Thailand. This is because Russia renewed its interest in promoting defence production and exports primarily under Putin's presidency and this policy will be continued under Medvedev. To promote the country's objectives, Russian leaders including Vladimir Putin, former Prime Minister Mikhail Kasyanov and others have made several visits to Southeast Asian countries.

Russia's keen interest in Southeast Asia was also evident in former president Putin's visit to Indonesia and his signing of an arms deal with that country. Its important to note that he was the first Russian leader to visit Jakarta since Nikita Khrushev visited back in 1960.

It was evident Putin wanted to renew and revive old political and economic ties with Indonesia.

These efforts seem to have yielded positive results. Lomo Corp delivered 50 portable SA-18 surface-to-air missiles to Vietnam under a US $64 million contract, Myanmar took delivery of dozens of MiG-29 fighter jets, and the Malaysian air force purchased a squadron of general purpose fighter planes as well as Sukhoi S-30K fighter planes from Russia. In addition, Russia supplies modern aircraft and helicopters to the region and has established technical maintenance centres in Malaysia and Indonesia, which means it is not selling only military equipment, but also providing services.

Similarly, to effectively deal with the destructive force of forest fires in tropical regions, many Asia-Pacific countries are keen to acquire Russian-made 'Be-firefighting-amphibious' aircrafts. Russia is also supplying KAMAZ trucks and many other civilian goods to the region. In the opinion of some defence experts, Russia has been able to achieve all these thanks to its permanent membership in the Asian regional organisations.

Conclusion

In conclusion it may be stated that Russia has re-emerged as a major global power. Under the former presidency of Vladimir Putin, Russia has become politically strong, with the concentration of power in the Kremlin, and has become economically strong and affluent with huge exports of oil and natural gas, and defence equipments. These factors have partly contributed to the growing assertiveness of Russia, both at home and abroad. There are strong indications that there will be continuity of these policies under the leadership of new President Dmitri Medvedev and Prime Minister Vladimir Putin.

Russia is facing a downward phase in its relations with the West. This is due to a variety of reasons. From Russia's perspective, Nato's eastward expansion is a threat to its security. There are also differences and misunderstandings between Russia and the West over many issues — the lack of a steady supply of Russia's oil and gas to West European countries, the issue of Russia's supply of nuclear equipment for power plants in Iran, the US decision to set up the Missile Shield in Poland, and so on.

The five-day Georgia-Russia War in August 2008 has worsened relations between Russia and the West, with uncertain consequences in the short term. All these factors have indirectly intensified Russia's 'Look East' policy with an emphasis on relations with China and Asean countries. Russia wants to re-assert its policy of balance of power with the West so far as the Asia-Pacific and the Asean countries are concerned. Russia claims to promote co-operation with Asean for mutual benefit in political, security and economic spheres. To achieve these objectives in the next decade or so, Russia intends to enhance its role in the Southeast Asian region, both through regional co-operation as well as through bilateral co-operation with individual countries.

With an emphasis on the increase in the production of military equipment and the modernisation of the defence sector, Russia will increase its exports of arms and equipments to Southeast Asian countries. Russia seems to be keen on strengthening ties in the defence sector, not only by increasing exports of defence equipment, but also through new forms of co-operation, such as establishing technical maintenance centres in Malaysia and Indonesia and so on.

Considering the fact that the share of its trade with Southeast Asia is not significant at present, Russia might take several measures to increase trade with these countries. It has the potential to export more oil and natural gas to some of the Southeast Asian countries. Russia's energy giants such as Gazprom and Rosneft, duly supported by the Russian state, might become more active in the energy sector in Southeast Asia and in the Asia-Pacific region in the next decade, through investments in joint ventures and acquiring assets in energy-related fields. Russia is keen to promote its national objective of enhancing its role as a energy super-power in the world.

Moreover, Russia seems to be keen on seeking the cooperation of Asean countries in various fields such as high-technology, banking and investment, development of the service sector, creation of SEZ and so on, fields in which some of them have developed considerable experience and expertise. Russia might also be interested in the participation of qualified and skilled work force from Southeast Asian countries in the economic development of Russia's Eastern Siberia and the Far East. This may help Russia reduce the proportion of the Chinese work force in the country.

While there is no likelihood of a return to the Cold War era, Russia would make all efforts to re-establish its position as an equal partner, with the United States, in world affairs. With vast potentialities of natural resources, world class technical expertise and the sustained high economic growth of the last few years, Russia might be able to enhance its political and economic power and position in the world, including in the Southeast Asian region.

References

Artyakov V. 'Russian-Indian Co-operation in Offset Projects.' New Theme on Russian-Indian Affairs. New Delhi, Sept-Oct 2006, p. 16.

Buszynski Lesszek. *Contemporary Southeast Asia. A Journal of International And Strategic Affairs.* Vol. 26, No. 2, Aug 2006.

Free Europe Radio Liberty Daily Reports Aug 15, 2008.

Gidadhubli, R.G. 'Putin's Economic Formula for Russia.' *Economic and Political Weekly.* Mumbai, Dec 8-14, 2007, p. 21.

Gidadhubli, R.G. 'Russia's Renewed Interest in Southeast Asia,' in Y.Y. Reddy (ed) *Emerging India in Asia-Pacific.* New Delhi, India: New Century Publications, 2007, p. 204.

Izvestiya, Moscow daily paper. 'Growing Energy Exports.' Nov 21, 2007

McFaul M. 'Re-engaging Russia: A New Agenda.' *Current History* Oct, 2004, p. 307.

Yevsei, G. 'Russian Fiscal Policy: Challenges Ahead: Beyond Transition.' *The World Bank Journal.* April-June 2007, p. 22.

9

Contribution of India and Russia to the Evolving International Order

For examining and evaluating the contribution of India and Russia to the evolving international order several questions arise. What are the factors that have contributed to the evolving international order? What are the positive and negative consequences in this evolving international order? How India and Russia can contribute in this evolving international order for their mutual benefit and for global benefit?

There are several factors which have contributed to the evolving international order. Firstly, the breakup of the Soviet Union and emergence of 15 sovereign and independent states about two decades back created new geopolitical, geo-economic and geo strategic issues for the evolving international order. Secondly, the Warsaw Pact communist block defence organisation ceased to-exist, while the rival -Western NATO institution of the capitalist block has not only survived but has also become stronger enlarging its membership with the admission of several former East European communist countries and even three Baltic States of the former USSR. NATO has been still vigorously pursuing its Eastward expansion policy creating conflict with Russia. Thirdly, there are new security related issues including energy security issue due to rising oil demand and price for oil and control over oil fields and oil pipelines. Russia and Central

Asian States are rich in hydrocarbon reserves and are producers and exporters of oil and natural gas to several countries in the world and particularly to many European countries. Fourthly, there is emergence of new regional organisations such as CSTO, ECO, SCO and their growing importance particularly of SCO which has major significance for the evolving international order. Fifthly, the process of globalisation during the last couple of decades has acquired great political and economic significance for movement of capital, technology and skilled manpower across the world. Sixthly, the recent international financial crisis has made deep impact on the evolving international economic order and there is realisation that economic gravity has shifted from West to East. Mention may be made of BRIC countries Brazil, Russia, India and China which are assuming great significance by virtue of their growing economic potentialities and high growth and prospects. Seventhly, there are some negative developments such as terrorism, ethnic conflicts, drug trafficking which adversely impact on the international order.

In this background it will be pertinent to recall the status of India and Russia in the international order. Both are large in size, possess huge natural resources, enjoy significant global political status, have huge economic potentialities and above all are known for long in human history. For post-Soviet Russia, communist ideology has become part of history. The process of transition from communist system to political democracy and market economy has been largely completed. Having attained political stability, Russia has demonstrated its capability as a major power regaining its status in regional and global security issues. In this evolving new international order, bipolar world has changed over to multi polar world and there is a qualitative change from super power rivalry to collaboration and cooperation (at times conflict) between USA and Russia. During the last two decades Russia has passed through various phases of economic development from economic crisis of 1990's to resurgence in economy during skyrocketing oil prices, had setback to economy due to global financial crisis followed by the present phase of economic recovery.

So far as India is concerned the concept of 'non-alignment' has become virtually irrelevant after the Soviet break-up. India has demonstrated its ability as a successful large democratic country in the world and a major power in the South Asian region. Both Russia and India are free from ideological fixation. Economic transition initiated by India in the early 1990's has qualitatively changed India's economy from middle-ranking power to emerging major economic power in the assessment of even international experts and political leaders. India's foreign policy has largely succeeded following policy initiatives of economic liberalisation facilitating fast economic growth. This is evident from a major economic indicator of foreign exchange reserves which jumped from about $ 2.2 bn in 1991 to over $ 200 bn at present, that is a rise of over 100 times in about 20 years. With sustained high economic growth during-last over a decade, Indian-economy was able to recover fast from the adverse effects of global financial crisis. Thus, from what is stated above it is evident that there is a paradigm shift in the international order as against what prevailed before the Soviet breakup about two decades back.

India-Russia Relations

It will be proper to analyze the contribution of India and Russia for the evolving international order in the background of India-Russia relations. India has time tested cooperation and friendship with the former Soviet Union and post Soviet Russia for the last several decades. It is true that in the opinion of Felix Yurlov, in the aftermath of Soviet break-up, it was not easy for Russia to immediately adjust to new conditions. This was due to major realignment of forces all over the world. However, by the end of the last decade under the premiership of Yevgenii Primakov Russia readjusted its focus and orientation giving due importance to the East in its foreign policy and strengthened its ties with Asian countries including India. This policy has been further strengthened during the last decade by the Russian leaders under the presidencies of Vladimir Putin and Dmitry Medvedev. It is important to note that India on its part had not made any drastic changes in its foreign policy orientation and was able to adapt to changing conditions. This was mainly because there was no ideological break in domestic policy nor was there any breakup of the country that Russia faced and suffered.

Be that as it may, overcoming such unavoidable circumstances, India-Russia relationship has acquired strength by encompassing all aspects— political, strategic, economic, social, cultural and diplomatic. Hence the relationship has grown into genuine strategic partnership not only on bilateral issues but also global issues. This is because the foundation of India-Russia multifaceted relationship is the commonality of interests both at national and international levels as expressed by the leaders of both India and Russia in their summit meetings held regularly over the last two decades. There is genuine commitment to building a multi-polar world order which needs to be pluralistic in nature and reflecting growing diversity in international relations. At the same time as stated by the Indian Prime Minister Manmohan Singh on the eve of summit meeting with the Russian leaders in 2009 both India and Russia have sought to respond to changes in the international system through different ways even while broadening their engagement with the rest of the world. Both share common objectives to challenge key issues including global economic crisis, energy security, terrorism, climate change and reform of global institutions of governance.

India and Russia have sustained decades of bilateral cooperation in economic and trade relations. In many fields such as metallurgy, heavy engineering, production of defence equipments, space technology and various branches of Science and Technology Soviet and later Russia's contribution has been significant for economic development of India. To recall steel and heavy engineering are classic examples of Soviet era economic cooperation which has greatly benefited India's economy. This is evident from the fact that Bhilai, Bokaro, Ranchi, Hardwar, Bhopal are living monuments of cooperation. The former USSR was the largest trading partner of India and in turn India among the developing countries was the most important trade and economic partner. In the evolving dynamics of international relations there are certain changes during the last two decades. To be specific, even as both the countries had sustained and high economic growth, except during international financial crisis, volume of trade and investment had been lagging behind. The bilateral trade turnover which reached the $7.5 billion mark in 2009 and the target of US$ 10 billion for 2010 is likely to be achieved. But this is well below the potential, given the size of the Indian and Russian economies. There is need and scope to widen the trade basket, and promote greater investments in each other's countries. As stated by the Indian prime minister pharmaceuticals, Information Technology and diamonds can become areas of future growth.

While Russia has been able to sustain its growth in exports to India, the reverse is not the case. Moreover, there are changes in the commodity composition of India's exports to Russia and major traditional items are no more important. On the other hand, in Russia's total basket of exports to India, the share of machinery and equipments continues to be high even at present. Vlad Grinkevich has opined that India is one of the few countries to which Russia exports mainly hi-tech goods. This is evident from the fact that in Russia's total exports to India in 2009 the share of heavy machinery was 46 percent; steel 12 percent; fertilizer 15 percent and so on. This was apart from Russia's huge defence exports to India which continues to be significant. All these facts taken together it need hardly be overemphasised that for Russia India is important for its own economic development and as a trading partner. Specifically exports to India have great importance for Russia which is reviving its economy in the aftermath of latest international financial crisis. Thus, the target of trade turnover is expected to touch the figure to $20 billion by 2015.

In the evolving international order there is considerable scope for promoting India-Russia ties in new areas such as Nano-technology, bio technology, Pharmaceuticals, Information Technology, Super computers etc. Interaction among scientists of eminent institutes of India and Russia has strengthened over the last couple of decades. Joint Industrial Research Centers of excellence have been established to pursue and promote advancement in S & T which will have international relevance. Notwithstanding these positive developments there is scope for more achievements if certain steps are taken. In the opinion of some experts S and T in Russia still operates on Soviet-era style where experts and scientists have no direct interaction and have to operate through bureaucratic channels and state organisations. Similarly, at present interaction and collaboration between India and Russia are mainly in defence related activities and there is more scope for cooperation in the civilian sector. Needless to state that in the era of globalisation and liberalisation scope and potentialities in the civilian technologies are very high as compared to existing level of interaction.

Pharmaceutical products are major items in India's exports to Russia and Indian pharma companies have made a good name and are cheap in the Russian market. Yet India's share is negligible about 3.2 percent in Russia's imports and hence there is scope for increasing India's exports if certain constraints are overcome. For instance, in the opinion of some experts dealing with India's exports of pharmaceutical products to Russia, the methods of testing pharma products in Russia are not modernised while methods used by India are modem and acceptable in USA and Europe. Yet even-leading-Indian-manufacturing and exporting firms in this sector face the problems of longer time required for registration of their products than European firms, which puts them at a disadvantage in terms of cost and time for exports to Russia. Equally important is that Russia has recently proposed that clinical trials be conducted in Russia for approval of products. India's generic products are about 60 percent cheap as compared to that of USA or West Europe and are of equally good quality. Hence Russia should take advantage of these factors so that its healthcare cost is reduced while promoting greater cooperation between the two countries in the pharma sector.

It is a matter of great significance that India and Russia have extended their cooperation in strengthening their position in respective regions. India in South Asia and Russia in Central Asia and East Asia which has enabled both the countries to interact more effectively in promoting larger geopolitical interests. This assumes importance considering the fact that some parts of South Asia and Central Asia including Afghanistan are characterised by social and political instability, religious terrorism which are affecting directly and indirectly both India and Russia. These are challenging tasks for both the countries which are facing formidable problems since both are victims of growing international terrorism and drug trafficking in the region.

India-Russia-China Triangle

More than a decade back Russia proposed the idea of forming Russia-India-China alliance. All the three countries are also part of the BRIC which is assuming considerable significance in evolving international order. The heads of the states of BRIC meet from time to time to review global political and economic situation. The tenth meeting of the heads at the financial conference was held in Brasilia on 15th April 2010, the timing of which was significant since Brazil, India and China had withstood the international financial crisis much better than Russia and there were skeptics who commented whether BRIC will turn into BIC. But Russian leaders have demonstrated their determination to recover and revive the battered economy for which economic cooperation with India, China and Brazil have also supported. Needless to add that rational policy of modernisation and diversification initiated by the Russian president Medvedev has immensely contributed for economic recovery.

India has been strongly and consistently supported by Russia in the Shanghai Cooperation Organisation in which it has observer status. Russia is also supporting India's status as a permanent member in this organisation. Terrorism and other security related issues emanating from Afghanistan and some parts of Central Asia are matter of great concern for all members of SCO and have assumed significance. There is realisation that to deal with global challenges there is need to address issues by cooperative effort and with participation of major and emerging powers and economies. Such groupings like G-20 and BRIC are the building blocks of the emerging global architecture and financial reforms. India and Russia have similarity of views on most of the global issues which enable them to coordinate closely in G-20 and BRIC.

Some analysts have apprehensions about the advantages-for India regarding IRC triangle. It is argued that this triangle is strategically inadvisable for India as China is a part of strategic nexus with Pakistan aimed at India. It is also opined that there is lack of level playing field between the two countries and that China would not concede India's preeminent status in South Asia. It is also argued that there are some prevailing conflicts of interests between India and China on various issues- territorial, border issue, influence over regions, competition in economic field, and 'strategic competition' in South Asia and Central Asia. This is rather a pessimistic view which could be partly based on the perception that China pursues policy of exclusive approach in its foreign policy. Russia has an overwhelming status in this IRC triangle. It is important that China needs to take inclusive and accommodative approach in its policies for strengthening trilateral ties and for the benefit of all partners of the Triangle and also for making positive and effective contribution for the evolving international order.

Expectations of improvement in the relations among RIC have become stronger subsequent to the outcome of the 10th trilateral meeting of foreign ministers held in Wuhan in China in November 2010. The three countries focused on plans for coordination of actions to develop an open and inclusive framework in the Asia-Pacific Region. The three emerging powers sharing similar views on various regional and international issues including security, combating international terrorism, cooperation in the field of economy, energy, information technology, etc. The three countries reiterated support to UN's core role in global affairs. Specifically the three foreign ministers of RIC called for joint action for combating terrorism and urged the UN member states to urgently conclude and adopt the Comprehensive Convention on International Terrorism. In the opinion o some analysts the fact that Russia has joined the East Asia Summit mechanism and Asia-Europe Meeting Forum whose participants include India and China, the three countries have an opportunity to more effectively cooperate and interact at such regional organisations for promoting the larger interest of evolving international order.

Notwithstanding substantial improvement in the relations, certain bilateral issues and problems have persisted at bilateral level between India and China. In this context the Indian foreign secretary Nirupama Rao stated in November 2010 that disagreements between India and China on certain issues can be discussed and resolved to ensure that the relationship between the two countries is strengthened. As per reported by *Times of India* on 1st December 2010 there is optimism in India in this regard and that the two major Asian states are going to be the most important in the Twentyfirst Century. India's national security advisor Shiv Shankar Menon has stated that the Chinese premier Wen Jiabao will have a 'landmark visit' to India in December 2010.

Russia- USA and NATO

Russia being part of super power during the Soviet era, has reemerged as a major political power after the Soviet breakup. Overcoming problems of transition, Russian 'leaders have demonstrated that Russia is politically stable, dynamie, strong state' to deal with domestic and regional issues even as some conflicts have cropped up from time to time. Notwithstanding certain hiccups, Russia has enhanced its role in global affairs by cooperating and strengthening relations with other major powers including USA, West Europe, Japan etc. So far as relations with the USA are concerned in the autumn of 2009 Russia and USA opened a new era in their relations by resetting the button. Subsequently, leaders of both the countries have been building on it by taking several major policy measures. The Russian president Medvedev and US president Obama deserve to be credited for successfully strengthening bilateral ties which have also global significance with their frequent visits during the last couple of years and at various summits including the recently held summits at G-20, APEC and NATO in October and November 2010.

A major development of international significance has been that Russia and USA signed an accord for new START in April 2010 which is expected to be approved by respective governments. This accord promises to reduce nuclear missiles that each of them hold by one-third which will also radically reduce global nuclear threat and help in evolving new international order. This accord is also significant since by reducing nuclear stockpile, both the countries are expecting to reduce their defence expenditure to promote and enhance economic development. Moreover, the US strong support to Russia's accession to WTO in October 2010 will promote Russia's role in international economic issues apart from helping modernize and diversifying Russia's domestic economy. In December 2010 the European Union has also decided to support Russia's entry into WTO in 2011. Russia is also seeking support of Western countries for its modernisation policy. During his meeting with the Italian Prime Minister on the 3rd December 2010, the Russian president Mededev stated "Russia is interested in all leading countries of the European Union taking part in the modernisation of Russia's economy. We need technology, skills, help with personnel. In this sense we expect that such kind of relations will develop with Italy". This has become possible with improved political and economic relations between Russia and the West contributing positively to the evolving international order.

Another development of international significance is that Russia-NATO ties have changed qualitatively after the Lisbon summit held on 20th November 2010. As opined by analysts cold-war era has officially ended and there are growing prospects that both will participate jointly in dealing with global security issues. The USA is a major player in NATO and hence the statement of the US ambassador to NATO Daalder is quite significant in the evolving international order. According to him, "NATO was rebuilding the alliance"'by 'Resetting' its relations with Russia. Hence NATO summit has historic significance as it dealt with important challenges of Twenty first Century including terrorism, missile deference etc. This assessment is further reconfirmed by the NATO Secretary-General Anders Fogh Rasmussen at the Lisbon summit who made an important historic statement on 21st Nov 2010. As per RFE/RL sources he said "The NATO nations and Russia have today agreed, in writing, that while we face many security challenges we pose no threat to each other," He added "That alone draws a clear line between the past and the future of NATO-Russia relations." This is of great significance to the evolving international order. Russia has already been extending cooperation to the West in its operations in Afghanistan by allowing Russian territory to transport equipments etc. to Afghanistan. There are even speculations of more active participation of Russia with NATO in its Afghan policy. NATO is a global actor and hence deals with global threats and global challenges. Hence with participation and cooperation of Russia, NATO seems to be confident to deal with new challenges. In this regard it is worth mentioning the statement of the Russian president Medvedev after the meeting of NATO-Russia Council in Lisbon on 21st Nov 2010 "Russia will jointly with NATO monitor the nuclear programmes of some countries, including Iran". This decision of NATO and Russia will make immense contribution to promote nuclear disarmament and to effectively deal with nuclear threats emanating from different parts of the world.

Energy Security in the Evolving International Order

Energy security issue is important in the evolving international order. India and Russia are cooperating on various issues which have not only bilateral but international significance. Energy sector is one such issue in which there is close cooperation between the two countries. As the Soviet Union in the past, Russia over the last two decades has played an important role in exploration and exploitation of oil, natural gas, coal in India. For instance, Russia's major energy firms Gazprom, Rosneft have been active in India's energy sector in the Bay of Bengal's Continental Shelf. Tumenneftgeofizika has jointly with Indian oil company has carried out exploration in Assam. In turn Indian oil company ONGC has been actively participating jointly with Russian oil firms in the oil exploration and exploitation in Russia's Far Eastern region of Sakhalin-1. This is an example of inclusive policy approach of economic cooperation which is helping both the countries. In the opinion of experts there is scope for Russian firm Stroitransgas with high tech experience in laying underground oil and gas pipelines can collaborate with Indian firms in the construction of underwater gas pipelines from Iran to India across the sea even bypassing Pakistan. This proposal has great potentiality to promote North-South Corridor linking Russia, Central Asian States, Iran and India to meet India's growing demand for oil and natural gas apart from enhancing trade opportunities.

It is important to note that considering that oil is a non-renewable energy, there is increasing role of nuclear power in meeting the growing demand for energy in India. In this regard India-Russia cooperation is unique in developing India's nuclear power sector. Kudankulam in Tamil Nadu is a classic example where atomic power plant uses reactor VVER-1000 for which Russia has provided credit and assured supply of uranium for 40 the next years. As stated by Igor Volkov this is the third-generation nuclear reactor and is certified as meeting the European Utilities Requirements (EUR) and that India and Russia have drawn 'Road Map' outlining plans to build more nuclear power plants in India during the visit of Russian prime minister Vladimir Putin to India in March 2010. Considering the fact that there will be growing energy demand in the coming decades both in India and in many countries in the world, nuclear cooperation between India and Russia is a positive development. In fact nuclear energy has already been assuming importance in the developed countries of West Europe and in meeting their energy needs. India not being endowed with hydrocarbon resources has to depend more on nuclear energy in the decades to come. In this context the Russian government has offered India a golden opportunity to meet its nuclear energy needs. As reported by Russia' RIA Novost on 21st Nov 2010, Rosatom spokesman Sergei Novikov made an important statement that Russia's state nuclear corporation Rosatom has offered Indian companies cooperation in development of uranium deposits in Russia and other countries. What is equally important for India is what Novikov's added "We have offered Indians a role in uranium extraction projects in Russia and in third countries. Rosatom should always retain control over the projects, partners may receive up to 49 percent of projects inside Russia".

At regional level both India and China are major importers of oil in the world market since their national domestic hydrocarbon resource potentialities are relatively limited for meet their growing demand. Hence in reality there is competition between India and China for acquiring energy resources overseas in Asia, Africa, Middle East and even in Central Asia. In the opinion of many experts China has been more successful than India since it has taken a lead in linking its energy security policy with its national economic policy longer than what India has been able to do. Considering the fact that new sources of oil become more difficult, there are bound to be areas of friction between India and China in the future. Russia being one of the largest producers of hydrocarbon resources and a major exporter in the world market can play an important role in this trilateral cooperative scenario. Russia has also significant influence over Central Asian States with regard to energy sector by virtue of the fact that Russian energy companies Gazprom, Rossneft, Lukoil etc have been actively operating in exploration and transportation of oil and natural gas to international market. Moreover, the Russian policy-makers having close and co-operative ties with the leaders in Central Asia might make positive contribution in this regard since it will also benefit them. Hence Indian efforts can succeed in getting oil from Central Asia with active support of Russia. What is also important is that China should adopt inclusive policy and not exclusive policy for the benefit of all the countries concerned. As opined by Valerie Titov at the 2006 "Strategic Dialogue" India and China had agreed to cooperate rather than compete for global energy resources. Hence this incipient Sino-Indian entente has a potentiality to alter Asian geopolitics significantly which can have positive influence for creating a new international order for economic growth in the Twenty-first Century.

In the evolving international order Russia's role has increased significantly. During the last over a decade there is a Great Game being replayed on the issue of energy security between Russia on the one hand and the Western countries on the other in exerting influence over energy sector in Azerbaijan and Central Asia. For instance, there is an ongoing conflict concerning South Stream Project and Nabucco Project. The South Stream project, in which Russia, Bulgaria and Greece are partners, stipulates the construction of a 300-kilometer pipeline from the Bulgarian Black Sea port of Burgas to Alexandroupolis on the Greek Aegean Sea coast. The pipeline is promoted by the Russian authorities as a rival to the Nabucco project. The 3,300 kilometer Nabucco pipleline (capacity of 31 billion cubic meters) will transport Central Asian gas to Europe through Turkey, Bulgaria, Romania, Hungary and Austria, bypassing Russia, while the South Stream pipeline (63 billion cubic meters) will carry gas across the Black Sea to Bulgaria. The European Commissioner for Energy Guenther Oettinger admitted on 22nd November 2010 that Russia's South Stream gas pipeline is a potential competitor to the EU-backed Nabucco project. Notwithstanding differences Russia is seeking cooperation of Germany which is Russia's major partner in its trade and economic relations. Germany is a consumer of Russia's hydrocarbon resources. As reported by Russian journal Kommersant the possible participation of a strong German partner in the Russian-Italian South Stream gas pipeline project could undermine the rival Nabucco pipeline by offering attractive terms. (RIA Novosti 14th July 2010). Thus, during the two decades Russia has been trying to emerge as energy superpower by exerting influence of controlling pipelines from Russia and Central Asia to Europe.

Advancement in S&T in the Evolving International Order

Advancement in Science and Technology has become crucial in the evolving international order. Russia's policy of modernisation is quite comprehensive encompassing political, economic and technical components. Technological development and diversification of economy are significant parts of the policy of modernisation. This assumes importance because as opined by several Russia experts the role of Russia has been largely reduced to be an exporter of oil, metals and raw materials and importer of finished goods of high technology. In view of this the Russian President Medvedev is very serious and has directed the concerned government bodies to speed up the process of implementation of his declared policy of modernisation. There are issues which concern Russia's policy which have international implications since they relate to the creation of proper investment climate and to attract foreign investment and technology. Hence as stated by the Presidential aide Arkady Dvorkovich on 29th November 2010 Russia will review intellectual property rights, customs regulation, export and currency control, immigration laws, as well as standardisation of technical regulations to ensure that the policy succeeds enabling the country to make effective role in international economic order. In order that projects of technical modernisation are not affected due to shortage of funds, Medvedev directed the government to spend at least 50 percent of the scheduled saved expenses as well as the part of the federal budget's additional incomes to be allotted for modernisation. Considering that modernisation process was not proceeding fast enough and being aware of the fact that a significant part of bureaucracy and business in the country had yet to realise that modernisation is a long term process, as reported by Novosti on 20th September 2010 Medvdev was candid in stating at Yarosavl "There is absolutely no alternative to modernisation of the economic or political system."

On the issue of advancement in S and T, there is a new era in Russia's relations with the West. With improved cordial relations with the USA, Russia has been able to make a major gain by getting the US support for its hi-tech IT sector by getting its own brand of Silicon Valley at Skolkovo near Moscow. This was possible subsequent to the visit of Medvedev to Silicon Valley in 2009. There has been considerable support from USA in this regard including during the visit of California governor to Moscow in the spring of 2010. With investment of over eight billion Rubles and expected investment from a large number of firms including Microsoft, Google and also from Japanese, Indian and UK firms apart from Russia's nuclear institutes, Russia is proud of its own Silicon valley in Skolkovo. The US software giant Microsoft Corp will establish a research and development center in the Skolkovo innovation hub near Moscow, which was confirmed by the Microsoft CEO Steve Ballmer and Skolkovo president Viktor Vekselberg. The Russian IT sector would be immensely benefited with the participation of Microsoft since the R&D center in Skolkovo would focus on the cloud computing technologies both for Russia and the rest of the world. What is more important is that along with the R&D center, Microsoft has proposed to establish an information technology testing center that would help IT specialists test their software products in various conditions. The US IT giant will also participate in creating Skolkovo University of Technology which would work in tight cooperation with Microsoft's divisions in Cambridge and Redmond. What is also beneficial for Russia is that as confirmed by the head of Microsoft Russia, Nikolai Pryanishnikov the Microsoft also plans to support one hundred Russian startups investing from $50,000 to $500,000 on each of them.

Skolkovo has great international significance for Russia and to make it a success, the Russian leaders are seeking cooperation and help from other advanced countries also by way of investment and technology. There is scope for Indian companies in IT sector to participate in Skolokovo for mutual benefit. It appears India's Tata Group of companies has already been considering participation in Skolkovo. Morever, as reported by Novosti on 15th November 2010 the foreign minister of Russia Serge Lavrov made an important statement in Wuhan China that the foreign ministers of Russia, India and China have decided to establish close contacts between their innovation centers to further develop their strategic partnership. Innovation hubs are already operating in India and China while Russia has recently announced plans to build an innovation center in Skolkovo to facilitate the country's transition to a knowledge-based economy.

These are positive developments which need to be realised with consistent efforts of major countries for benefit of all.

Conclusion

In lieu of conclusion it may be stated that Soviet breakup, emergence of several sovereign and independent states, end of cold-war era, globalisation, international financial crisis have brought about a paradigm shift in the evolving international order. India and Russia with their decades of time-tested cordial relations, cooperation for mutual benefit, commonality of views on various global issues have proved that their policies of peaceful coexistence and inclusive growth have great relevance for the evolving international order. Russia reemerging as a major political power opened a new era with the West and NATO. India as emerging economic power has made major contribution to shift economic gravity from West to East. Both have independently and jointly applied political and economic policies with their active participation in regional- and international organisations and even as certain problems and shortcomings persist, they have made positive contribution to the evolving international order and seeking rational solutions to various issues including energy security, advancement in S and T, nuclear threats, international terrorism for achieving durable peace and sustained economic development.

Sources

1. Felix Yurlov, 'Russia-India: Facing Together the Partnership Challenge' In the book *Indo-Russian Diplomatic Relations-sixty Years of Enduring Legacy* edited by P. L Dash and Andrei M Nazarkin Academic Excellence Delhi 2008.
2. Vlad Grinkevich, 'Russian-Indian Trade Increases Despite of the Crisis' p. 6 New Theme New Delhi September-November, 2009.
3. 'Russia, India, China to Establish Close Contacts between Innovation Hubs-Lavrov'. Wuhan 15th November 2010 (RIA Novosti).
4. R.G. Gidadhubli, 'Economics and Politics of Russia's Energy Exports' in the book *Resurgent Russia*. Ed by Dhandapani Alagiri The Icfai University Press Hyderabad, 2009.
5. A.M. Katre, 'Indo-Russian Cooperation in Science and Technology: Retrospect and Prospect. In the book *Indo-Russian Diplomatic Relations-Sixty Years of Enduring Legacy* op.cit

6. R.G. Gidadhubli and Sanjay Deshpande, 'India and Russia: Contretemps in Cooperation' in the book *Indo-Russian Diplomatic Relations-sixty Years of Enduring Legacy* op cit.
7. Sreemati Ganguli, 'Indo-Russian Relations- The Making of a Relationship: 1992-2002.Maulana Abul Kalam Azad Institute of Asian Studies Kolkata, SHIPRA, 2009.
8. Raj Kumar Kothari, 'Recent Trends in Sino-Indian Relations' in the book *India's Foreign Policy in the New Millennium Ed* by Raj Kumar Kothari pub by Academic Excellence, Delhi, 2010.
9. Ranjana Mishra, 'Changing Contours of Indo-Russian Strategic Relations' in the ed book *Indo-Russian Diplomatic Relations-sixty Years of Enduring Legacy,* op cit.
10. Ajay Patnaik, 'Energy Geopolitics in Eurasia' in the book *Globalisation and Eurasia* ed by Ajay Patnaik and Tulsiram KW publishers Pvt Ltd. New Delhi, 2010.
11. Arun Mohanty, 'Russia's Socio-Economic Development strategy upto the year 2020- An Analysis' in the book Ed by Ajay Patnaik and Tulsiram op cit.
12. Maria Selivanova, 'Anti-Crisis Pill' New Theme, New Delhi, January-February, 2010.

10

Embargo versus Sanction: Tit for Tat between Russia and the West

A NEW COLD WAR?

In the first half of August 2015, the Russian Government declared its policy of embargo on imports of food products such as fruits, vegetables, cheese, poultry items etc from the Western countries. In early summer Russia initiated a campaign against foreign foods and subsequently enforced a ban on imports. This was a reaction to the policy of economic sanctions imposed by the West on Russia for its alleged involvement in the east Ukrainian conflict and for its annexation of Crimea in August 2014. While this was assumed to be a routine reaction of Russia towards the West, the situation has worsened attracting global attention. Hence an effort has been made here to examine as to why the issue has become serious, what are the factors impacting on Russia and the West and whether Russia will succeed.

Firstly, Russia has been quite serious with its policy-decision of embargo and hence has declared that those caught importing food products would face imprisonment of up to seven years. Russia's keenness to strictly and swiftly, implement its policy-decision is evident from the fact that as per the statement of the Interior Ministry, six members of an alleged mafia involved in a cheese-smuggling ring were arrested on August 23 as they possessed 470 tonnes of forbidden cheese.

Secondly, as per the presidential decree, imported food should be destroyed and what is equally significant is that the destruction should be supervised by two government officials and verified by photos and videos, which indicates that there is foolproof of banned food being destroyed. There are many instances of implementation of this policy by Russian officials during the last few weeks. For instance, on August 6, 10 tonnes of contraband foreign cheese were steamrolled outside Belgorod on the Russian- Ukrainian border. As reported by Radiqvesti on August 6, in Altai, near the Kazakh border, some 100 kilos of apples from the Netherlands, mushrooms from Poland and kiwis from Italy were also destroyed. Again, as stated by the Russian officials, on August 24, 600 tonnes of illegal food had been destroyed and these included fruits, vegetables, cheese, frozen Hungarian geese etc.

While Russia has the legal right to prevent illegal imports, destroying these products has been criticised by some analysis since over 16 million Russian alive below the poverty line. The lower and low middle class, constituting about 45-50 per cent of the total population, cannot afford fruits, meat, cheese etc. Hence the rationality on such an action is being questioned and, as rightly opined by some analysts, the Kremlin is sacrificing the welfare of Russians for the sake of patriotic propaganda.

Thirdly, as opined by some analysis, there were reports of burning of 1.5 tonnes of food imported for a BMW racing team which was to take part in Moscow on August 27. This is highly irrational and crazy and hence might have adverse consequences for the international event in which many foreign sportspersons were to take part.

Fourthly, initially Russia imposed a band on imports from the USA and European Union countries. Subsequently, the number of countries had been increased to cover Australia, New Zealand etc. For instance, in the third week of August the Russian Prime Minister, Dmitry Medvedev, added four more countries, namely, Albania, Montenegro, Iceland, and Lichtenstein banning import of food products. This reiterates the decision of Russia to hit back at the West for their economic sanctions on Russia. Similarly, Russia has imposed visa restrictions on select US officials in retaliation of restrictions imposed on Russian bureaucrats, officials and industrialists.

Fifthly, Russia seems to be bent on imposing import restrictions not only on food products but on non-food products as well from the West. Thus, the network of embargo products has widened and the process has become pervasive; this is evident from the fact that on August 25, Russian authorities ordered stores across the country to remove Western brands of popular washing detergents and soaps from the shelves. But this might become counter-productive and adversely affect the popularity of the government. What was highly controversial was preventing access to Wikipedia on August 24, and this did create panic in the country and became hot news all over the world against Russia. But good sense prevailed as it was lifted by Roskomnadzor a few hours later.

Sixthly, Russian authorities seem to be on the warpath on the issue of embargo. The Russian Consumer Protection Agency claimed on August 25 that recent inspections of selected goods of top foreign brands such as Colgate-Palmolive and Procter and Gamble have high levels of toxic ingredients and hence have begun removing household products from stores, claiming health risks.

The Western critics are amazed by the fact that Russia is finding fault with the quality of Western imported products such as soap detergents and cosmetic items which have become household products of Russian women and been used for decades.

It may be stated that in general Russia does not enjoy high reputation of producing high-quality consumer products and hence has been a major importer of these consumer goods even during the Soviet era. Thus, some Western critics call this as craziness and even question the timing of such actions considering the fact that these are well-known brands in the global market. What could be a contentious issue is the fact that the Russian embargo also includes items produced by the Russian company Nevskaya Kosmetika established in Russia; it is a joint venture with a Western firm.

Impact and Consequences

The question arises as to whether there is justification for such strong policy-decisions being adopted by Putin's Russia. There is no doubt that this will be a very contentious policy-issue among the critics and analysts of Russia and about the likely impact and consequences.

Firstly, a Moscow priest and commentators, including Yevgenia Nazarets, Aleksandr Gostev, were highly critical of destroying food and urged that it should have been used for feeding the poor and elderly people in Russia. Moreover, thousands of Russians signed online petitions urging Putin to cancel his latest decree and warning of potential consequences of playing with food issues amid economic crisis in the country. Russian analyst Savelyeva has opined that by August 6 about 280,000 persons signed a petition against the banning of food, but Kremlin spokesperson Dmitry Peskov questioned the validity of the signatures.

Secondly, while during the last couple of decades the objective of the Russian Government has been to integrate with the global economy and attract Western firms to produce and invest in Russia, there seems to a U-turn now by the Russian authorities on this issue which may have long-term adverse effect on the investment climate of the Russian economy and technology transfer from the West.

Thirdly, in fact in 2015 the Russian economic growth has been declining and has been facing recession due to the sharp global decline in oil prices (Russia being largely dependent on petrodollars by exporting oil and gas to the West European countries). The Russian economy shrunk by 2.2 percent in the first quarter of 2015 and the value of the ruble collapsed, causing inflation to rise to an annual rate of 16 percent.

Fourthly, Russia has been facing an acute shortage of food products including vegetables and meat etc. Prices have skyrocketed and a large section of people are unable to buy food products! Russia has been a major importer of meat and milk products as was the case during the Soviet era. In 2014 imports constituted about 30 percent of the total demand of milk products.

Moscow's embargo of Western food imports contributed to soaring food prices that rose by more than 20 percent by July, according to official statistics. The price of some staple goods, such as cabbage, rose more than 60 percent in early 2015. Hence Russian analyst Savelyeva is candid in stating that in Russia "people can't even afford the most basic food". That is why she says Putin's order to destroy food has been most unwise in Russian history. Hence under these circumstances, banning imports might aggravate social discontent and badly affect Putin's popularity.

Counter-arguments Favouring the Decision

While there could be arguments against this policy of embargo on imports from the Western countries and on the issue of destruction of banned food products, as per the survey by the Levada Center and by the All-Russian Center for Public Opinion Research (VTsIOM), public opinion polls conducted in August seem to be more or less equally divided. This could be a consolation to the policy-makers.

Commenting on and implicitly justifying the policy-decision of the Russian Government, Russian economist Vladislav Inozemtsev, Director of the Moscow-based Center for Post-Industrial Studies, has contended that Russia is heading towards an era of austerity and autarky at a time when thousands of domestic private and state sector enterprises are expanding.

Russia has the right to increase its domestic production and be self-reliant in food production and it claims to have already made some progress in this area. Russia has adopted the policy of 'Doctrine of Vegetable Independence' under which by 2030 about 86 percent of vegetables should be produced in Russia itself. As opined by Elena Turrina, Director of the Institute of Agrarian Marketing, there is some positive impact of embargo on investment activities to produce vegetables etc. in Russia itself and it may take about three years to feel the impact of the same. Hence while this could be a long-term perspective, there are differences in the estimates about the quantity and quality of domestic production. While, as per some analysts, during the year 2014-15 domestic production of milk has increased by only about seven percent, official sources claim that there was an increase of 24 per cent. In 2013 import of meat constituted about 25 percent of the total market of Russia and that has gone down to 18 percent in 2014. Hence to a great extent domestic production has picked up.

Political Strategy

It is important to note that Russia seems to evolve a deliberate policy of changing suppliers of food and other products. Traditionally the USA accounted for about 60 percent of the total import of meat and the EU countries about 25-30 per cent. As a result of contra-sanctions, import from these countries has been totally stopped. In their place Brazil and Argentina have emerged as suppliers of these products.

BRICS countries seem to get preference in the Russian market. For instance, Brazil is replacing the USA and Western countries for importing meat and poultry products. In fact, Belarus has overtaken Brazil as supplier of meat and poultry products to Russia. India has emerged as one of the new suppliers of meat products to Russia and at relatively cheaper rate as compared to, say, the European countries. While Egypt and Azerbaijan take the lead in exporting vegetables to Russia, Turkey has become another source of supply of vegetables and fruits to Russia.

Russia-Ukraine relations are on test. It is important to note that Ukraine has traditionally been a major source of import of pork for Russia. Now Russia has threatened to review its policy if relations do not improve in 2016. In the first half of 2015 Ukraine supplied 13,000 tonnes of meat to Russia, second to Brazil. It is important to note that there is a strong indication that in 2016 Ukraine would be added in the list of banned countries unless Kyiv reaches a settlement with Moscow that circumvents the economic regulations in Ukraine's trade accord with the EU.

In conclusion, it may be stated that Putin's policy of embargo has been controversial and is likely to have major consequences in Russia's relations with the West. Russian policy-makers assume their decision of banning imports will economically hurt these countries. While this seems to be highly optimistic, there are likely to be adverse impacts on Russia itself in the short term. Considering the fact that the whole issue of embargo is closely linked to Ukraine in which both Russia and the West have high stakes, and the crisis persists with no sign of an acceptable political solution emerging, a New Cold War may not be ruled out.

11

Cost and Benefit of Russia's Entry into WTO

In the third week of August 2012 the World Trade Organisation (WTO) admitted Russia as its 156th member. In fact, the Russian President Vladimir Putin, had added another feather on his cap as the leader of Great Russia by putting his signature on July 19, 2012 on the agreement ratified by the State Parliament (Duma) on July 10, for its accession to the WTO and thus ending Russia's ordeal of waiting for this event for about 19 years. By joining this economic organisation, Russia hopes to further promote its economic objective of integration with the rest of the world having already become a member of other. international economic organisations such as the G-8, G-20, AFEC. Major Western powers, including the USA, West Europe apart from India and China, who have strongly supported-Russia's case for accession, welcomed this event. As a token of support to Russia joining the WTO, the US Senate panel on July 19, 2012 voted in favour of lifting the Cold War era Jackson-Vartik Bill which restricted trade with the former USSR and post-Soviet Russia.

But inside Russia itself there have been protests by the Opposition parties and several leaders, including those of the Communist Party who voted against the agreement in the Duma, as Russia entered into its final stage of complying with the conditions of joining the WTO. Hence it is worthwhile to analyse and understand the cost and benefit of Russia's accession to the WTO and what challenges that lie ahead for the Russian leaders to achieve their economic objectives.

The basis for opposition and reservation to the accession to the WTO by certain political parties and leaders within Russia are as follows. First Nikolaev Arefev, a member of the Communist Party of the Russian Federation, alleged that the WTO is the 'Economic NATO[7] since it insists on liberalisation and free of trade which will worsen the position of Russia that 'hardly produces anything and is a major importer of a large number of goods. Secondly, the Left Democratic Party leader, Yarpslav Niiov, was also critical of the WTO, entry of Russia since this step, in his opinion, will increase unemployment as the foreign companies might sack workers to make more profit. Thirdly, some critics have argued that Russia is entering the WTO at a wrong time when there is a Eurozone crisis and recession in many parts of the world and hence goods might be dumped in Russia benefiting those exporting countries at the cost of Russia.

Fourthly, the Opposition leaders and some critics have argued that the Russian industrial and agricultural output will decline sharply as in the case of Ukraine whose industrial production went down by about 40 percent in one year after joining the WTO. According to some analysts, the negative impact on the Russian economy might be to the tune of 8-9 trillion roubles up to 2020. These eontentions are used by the Opposition political party leaders, including Communist Party leader Gennadi Zyuganov who voted against the proposal in the Duma, asserting that the Russian market could be captured, the agro-industrial sector will be put to toss, banking and insurance sectors could be targets by international corporations.

It is important to note that the Russian Government, is not unaware of the cost and impact of the WTO entry. For instance, in the short-term when import tariffs are reduced, some branches of economy such as automobile, engineering might face competition from foreign firms. In the opinion of Mikhail Delyagin, the employment position will be affected in engineering, agriculture, light industry and food processing industry to the extent of 15 million workers. Russia's Minister of Economics Belousov also informed at the Duma session on July 9 that Russia might suffer a budgetary loss in the next two years to the extent of about 445 billion roubles due to reduction in import duties.

Hence while some observations of the Opposition leaders and critics are valid, the contentions with regard to the cost of entry into the WTO are exaggerated and several arguments are not valid. For example, to argue and allege that the WTO is an 'Economic NATO' is wrong and baseless. There are already 155 member countries in the WTO with varying levels of economic potentialities and differing levels of development. In fact by virtue of their membership and cooperation, they promote international trade and also their own economic interest and development. Hence such remarks against the WTO seem to be politically motivated.

In fact, Russia has already been paying a heavy price for not being a member of the WTO, but this is not conceded, by the critics and Opposition leaders. Due to non-membership of the WTO, Russia has been subjected to many restrictive measures resulting in heavy economic cost. For instance, penalty due to anti-dumping procedure to Russia costs about $4 billion every year. Russia can reduce this cost by joining the WTO. Hence the Russian Government had justification to expedite the ratification of the agreement.

For any country that enters the WTO, there is some cost and adjustment involved in complying with certain conditionalities. Russia, being a former communist country and a closed economy, was guided mainly by political considerations and interests in matters relating to both domestic economy and foreign trade and economic relations. During the last two decades some measures have been initiated to bring about a market economy and incorporate regulations stipulated by the WTO for its membership.

Benefits of Entry into WTO

The basis and arguments in favour of joining the WTO are as follows: First, the contention of a Communist leader that Russia has been dragged into the WTO during the period of crisis and that the West will get benefit at the cost of Russia is not valid. While it is a fact that the timing of Russia's admission into the WTO has coincided with the Eurozone crisis and economic recession in some European countries including Greece, Spain etc., for that Russia has no control and moreover, Russia's negotiations with the WTO were already in the final stages. On the contrary, in November 2011 Russian political leaders expected that the WTO entry might spur its economic development and World Bank experts also indicated a very optimistic scenario contending that Russia's membership could expand its economic growth by 11 percent in the long term. Hence the then Russian President Dmitri Medvedev, was quite satisfied with the decision of the Russian Government for joining the WTO. Hence having complied with the necessary formalities, the Russian Government signed the protocol for admission to the WTO on December 16, 2011. In view of this the accusation by the Opposition party leaders on the timing of admission is not valid. It is important to note that having signed the protocol in December 2011, the ratification of this document had to be completed by July 23, 2012 for Russia to become a full-fledged member of this organisation failing which the whole procedure, which is quite complicated and time-consuming, find to be repeated.

As regards the delay in Russia's accession to the WTO, there is an important factor while looking back. Russia applied to join the WTO in 1993, but the negotiations dragged on in the 1990s. During the first decade of independence although many Western countries, including the USA, supported Russia's admission, the Baltic states of Latvia, Lithuania (which were part of the former USSR) objected to Russia's admission to the WTO mainly due to their ongoing mutual political conflict of interests. Subsequently, during the last decade Russia's admission was further delayed after Georgia blocked Russia's membership bid following Tbilisi's -brief war with Moscow, over South Ossetia in 2008. Moreover, under the then prevailing economic crisis conditions, Russia had difficulty in complying with the conditionalities of the WTO. This is evident from the fact that by March 2011, according to Russian sources, even after nearly 15 years, negotiations on 14,000 items were still underway with 56 countries since the process of negotiations had been a lengthy and technically complex job.

Apart from that on Russia's delay for admission into the WTO, the leading American expert on Russia, Marshal Goldman, opined in

November 2011 that there were some political leaders and business firms and enterprises owned by Russian oligarchs who enjoy monopoly control in Russia that were against Russia's accession to the WTO since they did not want outside competition and thus lose their economic advantage. In fact, this happens in any country and Russia is not an exception. Hence the delay due to sabotage of the proposal by some vested groups was quite possible.

Secondly, Russia is partly responsible for the delay in its entry into the WTO, since it has often used the political whip in its trade relations even with the countries of the former Soviet Union. This has been the case with Ukraine on the issue of the price for oil and gas. Similarly, as noted by some analysts, on several occasions. Russia used health concern as a pretext and banned import of cheese from Ukraine, mineral water from Georgia in 2006, dairy products from Belarus in 2009, wine from Moldova in 2010 and so on. Moscow's health officials can still be able to ban such imports, says Stephen Woolcock from the International Relations Departrnent of the London School of Economics. But after joining the WTO, Moscow has to apply uniform standards to all trading, partners and provide scientific documentation to justify their action, since such matters are covered by the WTO's Sanitary and Phytosanitary Agreement (SPS). While temporary bans are possible, if proved otherwise there is heavy penalty for imposing these. To safeguard the interest of all trading partners, the WTO keeps an eye on trade policies and could put pressure on any country if it was found to be imposing politically motivated trade sanctions. Russian economist Andrei Portanski has opined that Russia should have joined the WTO long bade arguing that it is at present a highly discriminated country in the world and with accession to the WTO this limitation can be overcome for the benefit of Russian exporters and producers.

Thirdly, it is important to note that after joining the WTO, the country enters a three-year period during which the leadership has to take effective measures to liberalise its markets to conform to the WTO rules. In fact, this is a good enough period for Russia to complete the process of implementing economic reforms and changes in institutional structures to make the Russian economy competitive.

Moreover, the Russian leaders face a challenging task to cut import tariffs and open up key sectors of the economy to attract foreign investment.

Fourthly, in this era of globalisation there is a need and realisation for Russia to integrate with the rest of the world and become a market economy and embrace open competition. Hence Russia cannot afford to remain Isolated and continue to depend upon petro-dollars by export iof oil and natural gas. The problem for Russia has become more complex since under the prevailing recessionary conditions the global demand for oil and gas has declined and so also the international price at about $ 90-98 per barrel which will significantly affect income generation from export of oil and gas. This would have a worsening effect on the Russian economy since during the last two decades, under the policy pursued by the Russian leaders, the country has been over-dependent on export of oil due to which other branches of the economy have been neglected and are lagging behind. Hence for diversification and modernisation of the industrial sector, accession into the WTO is necessary and desirable. This is also the valid argument of the United Russia party leaders. So far as the agricultural sector is concerned, Russia suffers from the spill-over effects and continuity of the Soviet era policies and hence this sector is highly subsidised, suffers from low productivity, high wastages and hence in many regions farms make losses. Therefore, the WTO entry might bring benefits to Russian agriculture and improvements in this sector with better quality agricultural machinery and setting up agro-processing plants to cut down wastages and produce high quality products.

Fifthly, it is important to note that, with entry into the WTO and reduction in import tariffs, the Russian population, particularly those belonging to the lower and middle income groups, will benefit from larger imports of consumer goods and services of better quality at lower cost. Hence the members of United Russia and Ministers tried to argue in the Duma about these benefits for the country when the proposal was put for adoption in Parliament.

Challenges

There are, however, a few challenges for Russia in achieving its objectives on joining the WTO. For instance, after joining the WTO,

Russia hopes to benefit by the net inflow of the much needed foreign direct investment and that *is* what the government wants and what Putin spelt out in his presidential address on assuming office in June 2012. Many Russian entrepreneurs, who are millionaires and billionaires, have also parked their money outside. It is a challenging task for the Russian Government to give incentives in order to get back that money. Moreover, Russia should be able to attract Foreign Direct Investment from Western countries, which can help in the economic growth of the state Germany is the largest trading partner of Russia relying on which the Putin Government hopes to get major, investments in Russia. But Germany, being involved in salvaging its Eurozone partners such as Greece and Spain, the prospects of huge investments in Russia could be limited in the short term. However, there are possibilities that other countries, including the USA, China and India, could invest in joint ventures in Russia. For that reason .the Russian Government should be consistent in its policies to improve the investment climate, open up the economy and offer opportunities for setting up joint ventures in various branches, including hydrocarbon, engineering, IT, pharmaceutical, consumer goods sector, infrastructure development and so on.

Apart from getting FDI, Russia should be able to get advanced technology from the West This. is very important since, as underlined by certain analysts, in some sectors, including engineering,. the level of technology in Russia at present is virtually the same as it was,before the breakup of the Soviet Union. By overcoming this shortcoming, in the long run Russia will be a competitive economy and achieve its declared objective of modernisation and innovation which is very much needed. For instance, the objective of developing Skolkdvo near Moscow-expected to become Russia's Silicon Valley— could radically improve its competitiveness in the IT sector on a global scale. Russia has the advantage of a highly qualified skilled manpower which can benefit with better job opportunities and higher levels, of income for the younger generation of Russians. But Russia cannot inodernise its economy without free and liberalised exchange of trade, services and technology. For mat the Russian Government should pursue consistent and liberal economic policies, reduce state intervention and bureaucratic control and corruption to facilitate joint ventures with foreign partners in order to boost economic growth.

In view of what is stated above there is some cost Russia has to pay for entry into the WTO. This is mainly the cost for adjustment in the short term which will be more than compensated by the benefits for the country in the long run. Hence Russia should be ready to pass through a tumultuous period of economic challenges and adjustment; this also needs strong political will and support to ultimately achieve the economic objectives.

12

Complexities of Russia-NATO Relations: Growing Conflicts

Russia-NATO relations during the last two and half decades have been saga of more conflict and less cooperation. An effort has been made in this paper to highlight and examine major issues and problems that prevailed between Russia and NATO.

The latest event of conflict between Russia and NATO was in April 2016. In fact, it was a matter of great concern and significance that NATO-Russia Council (NRC) meeting was held on the 20th April 2016 after two years which had raised hopes and expectations of improvement in relations. The main agenda of the 20 April meeting of the diplomats was to reduce the risk of deadly military confrontations between NATO and Russia. But an incident involving a US naval destroyer close to Russia's border in the Baltic Sea has not only dashed hope but aggravated the situation. As per reports on the 12 April 2016, two Russian Su-24 warplanes buzzed a US guided-missile destroyer in the Baltic Sea. Subsequently, on the 14 April 2016 the US military reported another close encounter between a Russian warplane and a US Air Force reconnaissance plane over the Baltic Sea which was the second such incident within a week. The context of these incidents assumes significance since Russian warplanes buzzed the US Navy ship that was conducting joint exercises with the Polish military in the Baltic Sea. Hence on the 14 April 2016 the US Secretary of State

John Kerry was candid in stating that the Russian pilots' actions were "provocative" and "dangerous." In fact, he was not only very critical of Russia but even reminded that the US warship was in international waters. Hence he reiterated and cautioned that under existing rules of engagement between Russia and NATO, such actions by the Russian navy planes "could have been shot down." These incidents had created conflict and controversy on the eve of the proposed meeting.

Denying any violation on its part and not yielding to western pressure, Russian response has been equally strong resulting in the warning by the Russian military that it would respond with "all necessary measures" to any future incidents. In fact, it is important to note that Russia's Defence Ministry defended the actions of those Russian pilots, contending that they had respected all safety rules. Hence Russia's pessimistic response was evident from the views expressed on the 27 April 2016 by the Russian Defence Minister Sergei Shoigu at a security conference in Moscow that the 20 April 2016 meeting of the NATO-Russia Council "did not inspire optimism". He even tried to put the blame squarely on the West and NATO. In view of these circumstances, sense of conflict has aggravated between Russia and NATO reducing the hopes of cooperation.

Considering the importance of these incidents, it is worthwhile to examine the context of the event. As per some reports by the Western media, Poland and other NATO members in the Baltic contended that they were worried about an increase in the Russian military presence in its Kaliningrad enclave in the Baltic region, where Russia has been positioning longer-range surface-to-air missiles during the last few decades. Hence some East European and Baltic States claim that they are the most affected by this event and hence on the 15th April 2016, the foreign minister of Poland Witold Waszczkowski made a statement at a conference in Bratislava criticizing "Russia's activity is a sort of existential threat because this activity can destroy countries." It is ironical that this was an expression of anti-Russia feelings poured by the official of East European country which was once a part of not only the Socialist bloc but also of Warsaw Pact led by the former

Soviet Union to counter NATO. It is a matter of fact that Russia has been objecting to the US proposal to install anti-missile defence equipments in Poland and Czech Republic to counter Russia. However, on this issue there has been a more moderate statement by the Czech Defence Minister Martin Stropnicky who urged strengthening NATO cooperation but added that Russia "should not be isolated." At the same time Stropnicky was critical of Russia which has been actively "testing the defensive capabilities of NATO in the Baltic region."

Cold War-Historical Background

Looking back into history, Super Power rivalry that prevailed for decades during the cold-war era based on ideology between the Capitalist World led by the USA and the Communist World led by the former Soviet Union ended and formal contacts and cooperation between Russia and NATO started in 1991, within the framework of the North Atlantic Cooperation Council. In 1989 even prior to the Soviet breakup, Warsaw Pact led by Kremlin was dissolved and there were expectations by Russian leaders that NATO will follow suit since in principle there was no security threat and no ideological conflict that persisted for decades between the two Super Powers. But much against these hopes and expectations, NATO not only survived but expanded adding 12 new countries between 1999 and 2009. This was because in 1994 NATO evolved the concept known as 'Partnership for Peace' under which many Central, East European and Baltic states joined NATO even as Russia was not happy with this development and chose diplomatic policy of only 'Constructive Cooperation' with NATO. In 1996 Russia was critical for NATO's action in the conflict in Yugoslavia which led to its breakup. Notwithstanding this the decade of the nineties witnessed closer ties with Russia joining Partnership for Peace Programme with NATO on 22nd June 1994 and both powers signed Founding Act on Mutual Relations, Cooperation and Security at the NATO summit held in Paris on 27th May 1997. A Joint Permanent Council was created, providing a forum for wide ranging consultations which played a positive role in improving relations between the two. This was of major global significance since a roadmap was laid based on 'lasting and inclusive peace in the Euro-Atlantic area on principles of democracy and cooperative security'. At the same time there was controversy among analysts including some Russians who argued that even as NATO became much weaker in terms of its military capacity it has become much more difficult to manage.

Russia and Neighbourhood

It is worthwhile to examine Russia's relations with its neighbours and their impact on Russia-NATO relations. The Caucasian countries assume considerable significance for Russia. While Armenia has been a close ally of Russia, there are ups and downs in relations with Azerbaijan and Georgia. For instance, Georgia assumed significance due to Colored Revolution, 5-day war in 2008 and subsequent recognition of independence of South Ossetia and Abkhazia by Russia.

Notwithstanding these issues the present regime has been trying to improve relations with Russia which were strained a few years back. At the same time the Georgian Prime Minister Giorgi Kvirikashvili during his latest official visit on 25th April 2016 to Washington met the Vice President Joe Biden, World Bank President Jim Yong Kim and International Monetary Fund officials. He was candid in stating that Georgia would remain on a pro-Western path even as it restored some ties with Moscow since the future of his post-Soviet country rested with the European Union and NATO. In fact, he even stated this policy has been based on the "very clear will of [the] Georgian people". Hence Russia has to be prepared and concerned with NATO coming closer to its border in the long run. During the last over two decades in their own interest the USA and West Europe have been keen to establish close ties with Georgia and these countries. Armenia has been close and consistent in its relations with Russia.

So far as Azerbaijan is concerned in March 2016 a NATO delegation visited Baku and met Azerbaijan's defence minister Hasanov who has been keen to expand cooperation with NATO. On this issue Russia was not very much concerned since relations with Azerbaijan have been consistently close and in fact Azerbaijan has been spending a lot of money on buying weapons from Russia. Hence Russia has been aware that this visit was in line with national and security interest of Azerbaijan, in fact Azerbaijan has adopted a shrewd policy of close ties with Turkey as well with which military cooperation have been expanding during the last over two decades and a joint military industrial complex has been created and joint military exercises are held once every three months. At the same time the leaders of Azerbaijan have not set any goal of being a member of NATO. On the other hand, Georgia, Moldova and Ukraine which have set themselves this goal have been facing problems allegedly caused by Russia for these countries and have not been admitted to NATO so far.

Ukraine

Ukraine has assumed great significance in Russia-NATO relations which have already come under cloud during the last about two decades on few issues such as impact of Orange Revolution, differences on pricing for oil and gas and transportation of oil and gas to West Europe by pipelines passing through Ukraine etc. Equally important has been pro-western governments that have come into power which have reduced importance of Russia in Ukraine's policy perspective and its sphere of influence. This has also resulted in reduction of trade and economic ties between Russia and Ukraine.

Moreover, multiple crisis conditions such as allegations by the West of Russia's forcible annexation of Crimea by deploying military forces in March 2014 and on-going conflict in eastern Ukraine by separatists have been a turning point in Russia-NATO relations. This is evident from the fact that on the 1st of April 2014, there was a statement issued by NATO foreign ministers that announced it had "decided to suspend all practical civilian and military cooperation between NATO and Russia". NATO has strongly condemned Russia's actions and criticized that it was a violation of Ukraine's sovereignty. Subsequently, in September 2014, the NATO-Ukraine Commission adopted a Joint Statement that "strongly condemned Russia's illegal and illegitimate self-declared "annexation" of Crimea". Further it was contended that Russia's action has caused deliberate destabilisation of eastern Ukraine in violation of international law.

Not accepting any of these allegations, Russia's policy has been that annexation was legal on the basis of referendum. Moreover, Russia has consistently argued that conflict in eastern Ukraine is a part of civil war. At the same time to strengthen its hold on this region, Russian defence forces have deployed additional forces in Crimea as a part of beefing up its Black Sea Fleet. It has also redeployed nuclear capable Tupolev Tu-22M33. As a result there have been military encounters between Russia and the NATO countries to Cold War levels, with 40 dangerous or sensitive incidents recorded in the eight months of 2014.

Under East-West dilemma facing the country, the Ukrainian president Poroshenko preferred to join NATO as against the status of non-alignment policy pursued by earlier presidents. As per reports of 24th December 2014 the Ukrainian parliament Verkhovna Rada adopted a law which allowed the country to become part of a military bloc. Being concerned about these developments, the Russian Deputy Defence Minister Anatoly Antonov not only opposed such decision but threatened possible adverse consequences in its relations with Ukraine and prevailing cooperation with NATO. While this was a golden opportunity for NATO to come on the border of Russia, it made a diplomatic move stating that Ukraine had to comply with few conditions such as settling its territorial disputes, conducting a thorough overhaul of its military and entire governance system before having a feasible chance of joining NATO. While complying with these conditions would take few years, Ukraine was offered the status of 'key ally of NATO'. At the same time NATO has also said that any meeting with Russia would have to address the conflict between Ukrainian government forces and separatists in eastern Ukraine, which has killed more than 9,000 people since April 2014. The West accuses Russia of supporting the pro-Russian rebels that has been denied by Moscow. The Western countries and NATO in particular demand Russia to comply with following conditions—implementation of ceasefire deal in Ukraine, known as 'Minsk-2'; comply with international law and its international obligations and responsibilities; end its illegitimate occupation of Crimea; refrain from aggressive actions against Ukraine; withdraw its troops; halt the flow of weapons, equipment, people and money across the border to the separatists; and stop fomenting tension along and across the Ukrainian border. Since Russia under Putin's leadership is most unlikely to comply with any of these conditions, conflict will persist at least in the near future.

East Europe and Baltic

In 2008 partly in the aftermath of Russia-Georgia war of 2008 some East European states including Poland, Czech Republic were keen to have antimissile NATO defence system on their territory for ensuring their security, while Russia was against NATO eastward expansion as it would threaten its own security. But from the perspective of the leaders of East European states, security situation was not totally normal. Hence in February 2010, Romania announced a deal with the USA for setting up an anti-missile defence system, which Russia interpreted as a threat to its national security. All these developments indicate persisting security related differences between Russia and East European states which were at one time close and part of military block. In this regard in 2009 Barack Obama cancelled the former decision of USA of installing missile equipments in East Europe possibly hoping to improve ties with Russia whose then president Dmitri Medvedev was also reciprocating with his reset policy towards Washington.

It is interesting to note that even as many East European states are close to West European democratic political system and have close economic ties with the European Union (EU) and NATO, in Serbia there is a strong movement by a political group which is keen to have close relations with Russia. As reported in December 2015 this organisation has announced the launch of an anti-NATO and anti-EU campaign and a return to Serbian nationalist ideology and the revival of the Radicals' original programme, oriented around closer relations with Belgrade and Moscow. It also advocates the protection of Serbian national identity and language and Cyrillic script in Montenegro. This was highly exceptional among the European countries but welcomed by Russia.

During the last few years, Baltic region and Nordic region have assumed significance in Russia-NATO ties. Estonia which was a part of the former Soviet Union became a member of NATO in 2004 followed by other Baltic States, namely, Latvia and Lithuania.

In April 2015 with growing tension in the Baltic region there was indication that these states could increase ties with NATO which Russia was highly concerned. It is important to note that both Finland, which borders Russia and Sweden are not members of NATO but have increased cooperation with the transatlantic alliance. From the perspective of leadership of Finland security situation in the region drastically changed after the crises in Georgia and Ukraine. With large Russian minorities living in the Baltic States, concerns had grown in the region about the risk of Russian intervention. In fact, amid such concerns, Estonia had called for a NATO force to be stationed permanently in this Baltic country. In that context in an article on the 9th April 2015 in Norwegian daily *Aftenposten*, the Nordic defense ministers expressed their concern claiming that Russian leaders had shown they were ready to use military means to achieve political goals. Hence under such prevailing circumstances, leaders of some European countries including Poland, Baltic States expressed their concern due to growing differences between nuclear powers of Russia and NATO. In fact, even Norway's defence minister Ine Eriksen Soreide opined that Russia had "created uncertainty about its intentions".

Possibly to make positive response to support these leaders, the United States and NATO have proposed to recalibrate and increase their presence in East European countries and Baltic States in 2016. Thus, US administration has already announced that it would quadruple defence-related spending in Europe and would increase the number of combat brigades rotating Eastern Europe. In fact, the latest incidents in the Baltic Sea involving a Russian plane flying close to US plane in April 2016 have been an added factor.

In this regard it is important to note that in the second week of February 2016 a western analyst Sam Jones in Munich stated that the Organisation of Security Cooperation of Europe (OSCE) played positive role monitoring the compliance of NATO states and Russia with the collection of cold war-era treaties and mechanisms that governed military bases, deployments and exercises in Europe. He mentioned that in 2015 Moscow unilaterally withdrew from the Conventional Forces in Europe (CFE) treaty, one of the diplomatic arrangements that the organisation had helped to implement, citing

NATO provocations. On this issue Dmitry Medvedev, Russia's prime minister was candid in stating that the world had stumbled into a "New Cold War". Strongly supporting this view Dmitry Solovyov opined that while NATO has been accelerating its biggest military build-up in Eastern Europe since the Cold War, the Western alliance wants to talk to Moscow about improved military transparency under the pretext of avoiding misunderstandings, which is highly contradictory.

Geopolitics

From what has been stated above, it is worthwhile to make an overview of geopolitics of conflicts and cooperation in Russia-NATO relations. During the major period of the nineties, Boris Yeltsin's pro-West policy and dissolution of Warsaw Pact created an environment of co-operation in Russia NATO relations. But hopes and expectation of Russian leaders that NATO would be dissolved remained a pipe-dream and expansionist policy of NATO led to disillusionment though not conflict in bilateral relations. In the first term of presidency from 1999-2003, Vladimir Putin actively pursued policy to develop cordial relationship with NATO and even proposed in 2001 policy for enhancing bilateral ties on 'Equal Footing'. Moreover, as a part of policy of continuity of cooperation, in 2002 NATO-Russia Council (NRC) was set up. However, apart from security related aspects, on issues of Soft-Power there were differences in perceptions between Russia and West including NATO powers. This was possibly because as opined by some western analysts, 'Putinism' combined state capitalism and authoritarian nationalism and even Eurasianism. Hence from western perspective this was against western values of democracy, freedom, liberalism etc. Notwithstanding that there was some improvement in bilateral relations under the presidency of Dmitri Medvedev. In 2009-2011 he bought about some rapprochement and cooperation in Russia's relations with the West and NATO. This was also facilitated primarily by the positive reciprocity between the US president Barack Obama and Medvedev when 'Reset' policy prevailed in bilateral relations. This was evident from the fact that, as mentioned earlier, in September 2009, Obama gave up US policy decision of missile defence installation in Poland and Czech Republic that Russia had firmly objected. Further in March 2010, Russia and USA concluded new 'START' treaty subsequent to which Russia cancelled sale of air defence installations to Iran. In response Russia extended total support to the USA in the aftermath of 9/11 attack and 'Global War on Terrorism'. This helped Russia not only to avoid isolation but also enhanced cooperation with NATO. It is important that NRC meetings were resumed coinciding the 60th anniversary of NATO which were stalled after Russia-Georgia war in 2008. In response Russia reciprocated transit of military hardware of USA to Afghanistan. However, as opined by some analysts, 'Reset policy' had mixed reactions among some European states. For instance Poland, Baltic States were not in favour of this policy since from their perspective Russia remained a potential threat to their independence. On the contrary, West European countries namely, Germany and France had been supportive of improved relations between Russia and NATO.

Possibly being disillusioned and discouraged by lack of positive response from the West to Russia's policy initiatives of cooperation including proposal of 'Equal Footing', assertive Vladimir Putin decided to bring about changes in Russia's policies towards the West. This is evident from the major shift in Russia-NATO relations during the last few years. For instance, Vladimir Putin nullified a 2011 order that created an interagency working group inside Kremlin that focused on fostering missile defence collaboration with NATO. He also revoked in April 2012 presidential decree that created a special envoy for missile shield discussion with NATO held by deputy prime minister Dmitry Rogozin. Moreover, in 2013, Putin deepened air defence cooperation with Belarus and Kazakhstan by sending additional S-300 missile defence systems to develop countermeasures to evolving NATO missile shield. At the same time possibly to strengthen Russia's position, in October 2013 Vladimir Putin rescinded two government orders concerning Russia-NATO relations. Putin's shrewd political diplomacy is evident from the fact that in April 2014 when there was a change in the headship of NATO, Putin despite strained relations with the outgoing NATO head Anders Fogh Rasmussen, welcomed the selection of former Norwegian Prime Minister Jens Stoltenberg as its new head with whom he had "very good relations". At the same time he expressed his frank opinion that it was up to the Western powers and NATO to improve ties with Russia.

At the same time most important development has been Putin's decision to strengthen Russia's military capability. On 26th December 2014 Russian President Vladimir Putin approved a New Military Doctrine. Prior to that, he had declared that Russia had to undertake military reforms in the security interest of the country. In fact, this was the fourth such declaration on national security following the ones that were adopted in 1993, 2000 and 2010. The main contents of Putin's Military Reforms were -Need for Russia to improve military capacity; Prevent NATO eastward expansion; Build up military forces near Russia's eastward border; Improve Russia's Information and Communication warfare; Fight against global terrorism. Hence the impact of this reform on Russia-NATO relations is important. On this issue Russian military expert Aleksandr Khramchikhin had been candid in replying to correspondent Nadezhda Kevorkova that Russia would not cooperate with anybody and that Russia's military reforms were always launched in connection with some possible events outside the country, At any rate Putin's military reform assumed geo-strategic significance in the context that Russia has been alleging that NATO alliance continued a 'Containment' policy towards Russia.

Hence from Putin's perspective this was part of *tit-for-tat* actions that have been undertaken by NATO. Hence Putin approved a revised national military doctrine to enhance its military capabilities in Black Sea region and even Baltic Sea region claiming that it was in response to NATO's military buildup near the Russian borders as the top military threat. For instance, in early February 2015 NATO diplomats expressed concern over Russia's nuclear strategy. In response Russia, cited NATO's *de facto* breach of the 1990 Treaty on Conventional Armed Forces in Europe. In June 2015 during his official visit to Estonia, the US Defense Secretary Ashton Carter declared that the US would deploy heavy weapons, including tanks, armoured vehicles and artillery, in Bulgaria, Estonia, Latvia, Lithuania, Poland, and Romania. This policy decision was interpreted by Western commentators as marking the beginning of a reorientation of NATO2's strategy. Reacting to this Russian Defense Ministry official condemned, this as the most aggressive act by Washington since the Cold War. At the same time it is important to note that even as NATO suspended all military and civilian cooperation with Russia in the aftermath of Crimean crisis in 2014, NATO authorities took positive diplomatic decision of continuing political dialogue with Russia. Equally important has been that both agreed to cooperate in dealing with problems of global significance such as fighting terrorism, drug trafficking, issues relating to disarmament and non-proliferation of mass destruction.

A Russian military analyst remarked that in the last two years, there has been a total change in this part of the world and security treaties and mutual-trust measures that prevailed earlier have ceased to exist. Hence on 16th June 2015 Russian news agency quoted Russian Deputy Foreign Minister Aleksey Meshkov who stated "none of the Russia-NATO programmes that used to be at work, are functioning at a working level." In fact on several instances Russia-NATO relations are strained during the last few months. For instance, as reported by Russia analysts on 24th November 2015 tensions rose when Turkey shot down a Russian warplane. It was alleged by the West that it had violated Turkish airspace while on a mission in northwestern Syria. But Russian officials denied that the plane had entered Turkish airspace. Similarly, Iran being a close ally of Russia got commitment of shipment of S-300 missile and radar equipments in April 2017 after Putin lifted the suspension of military supplies, which was frozen in 2010. This has raised strong objection by the West including frank exchange of views in the UN Security Council. While the Western powers argue that this will upset regional balance of power, Russia supported Iran's contention that this military power was purely for defensive and deterrent purposes.

The western reaction to Russia's geopolitics is evident from the concern and policy priority of USA for this region. The US president Barack Obama while addressing European leaders on the 25th April 2016 urged them to ensure unity among the states of European Union (EU). He even contended that the Russian President Vladimir Putin was trying to undermine the unity of EU. Possibly this was in the context of prevailing view of Britain leaving the EU after June referendum. The US president was also perhaps concerned about the threat posed by terrorism, and an ongoing refugee crisis that have tested European unity. Equally significant was that he underlined that NATO had to bolster its "front-line allies in Poland, in Romania, and in the Baltic states" while also meeting "the threat of its southern flank", his view of these circumstances he urged members of the EU alliance to increase their defence capacities and contribute their full share to the alliance and not become complacent about its own defence. More importantly, the underlying geopolitical objective of Obama was to put pressure on Russia accusing it for crisis and instability prevailing in Ukraine and forcibly taking over of Crimea in 2014. In fact, the USA and some Western countries are hell bent to punish Russia which has been reeling under economic sanctions by the West during the last about two years and declining oil prices, which have badly hit its economy very badly.

In the first week of May 2016 the US Army General Curtis Scaparrotti has been appointed as the new supreme commander of NATO who has stated on 4th May 2016 that his appointment has come at a time when the NATO alliance regards Moscow as a threat to stability over its actions in Ukraine and has largely given up on military or civilian cooperation with Russia. He has frankly stated that to strengthen NATO presence in the region he will urge Washington to strengthen defence capability and station a third permanent brigade of US troops in Europe to bolster the two brigades presently deployed in Germany and Italy. As opined by a western correspondent, Scaparrotti's most immediate challenge could be to lay down a clear boundary beyond which NATO units will not tolerate mounting harassment by Russian forces. He was candid in stating "Even with the end of the Cold War, our NATO alliance remains vital as we face a new set of challenges" identifying one of them as "a resurgent Russia, striving to project itself as a world power." In fact, Scaparrotti has been highly critical of Russian warplanes routinely buzzing NATO warships in the Baltics and the Black Sea during the last over a year. What is alarming is the fact that both NATO and Russia have stepped up military exercises in response to the Ukraine crisis. Moreover, from the Western perspective the latest event of close flybys by Russian war planes have created growing concern for the West and that they could lead to a direct confrontation.

Russia's reaction and response to policy declaration by Scaparrotti have been equally assertive. This is evident from the fact that on the 4th May 2016 Russian Defense Minister Sergei Shoigu announced that Russia will set up three new military divisions in the west and the south of the country by the end of 2016. This move was a response to what he called "the buildup of NATO forces in proximity to Russia's borders," as well as "intensified exercises of NATO countries." Hence there are possibilities of more conflicts between Russia and NATO in the near future.

Conclusion

From what has been stated above, following concluding remarks are made. Initiatives and policy decisions of Russia to dissolve Warsaw Pact, 'Constructive Cooperation', Founding Act on Mutual Relations and Reset-Policy played an important role for promoting cooperation between Russia and NATO. But pursuance of policy of Eastward expansion of NATO on misplaced perceptions of threats from Russia, refusal to accept Putin's proposal of 'Equal Footing' with NATO, problems arising out of Russia's relations with Georgia and Baltic states, impact of 'Colored Revolutions', allegation of annexation of Crimea by Moscow, persisting differences on Crimean issue and accusation for east Ukrainian crisis, economic sanctions to punish and weaken Russia have been responsible for ongoing conflicts between Russia and NATO. While there is urgent need for cooperation between Russia and the West to deal with problems growing terrorism in many parts of the world, drug-trafficking in the contemporary world, there are growing conflicts and complexities in Russia-NATO relations which are of global concern.

13

Trump-Putin Helsinki Summit: Advantage Russia

On July 16, 2018 the summit meeting held in Helsinki between Russian President Vladimir Putin and the US President Donald Trump was an important event from the bilateral and global perspectives. Several questions arise. What was the significance of this summit? What was the outcome of the summit? What were the responses and reactions to the outcome of the summit in America and Russia? An effort has been made to seek answers to some of these questions.

At the outset it needs to be stated that the summit was significant because the bilateral relations between Russia and America have been battered in recent years with confrontations and crises on several issues. There are allegations against Russia on the US election meddling, conflict in eastern Ukraine, Russia's alleged annexation of Crimea, nuclear arsenal, NATO and the war in Syria. American political leaders and media were putting pressure on Trump to raise these issues at the summit and seek answers from Putin. Hence on July 15 under growing opposition and pressure from various sources in the USA. Trump stated that he did not have high expectations from his meeting. "I go in with low expectations" and "maybe some good" would come out of the meeting. At any rate how many of the issues were discussed between Trump and Putin in their 'one-to-one' meeting are not fully revealed.

It is a known fact that Putin and Trump have met several times and know each other. Putin has mentioned that he has talked with Trump on phone several times. Hence some critics opined that Trump will be friendly to Putin and to Russia in general. This is in contrast to some American leaders who consider that Putin is an 'enemy' of America. But Trump has disagreed and asserted that Russia is a "competitor", not an "enemy" and has touted the summit as an opportunity to reduce tensions between the two countries.

One issue that has hit the headlines is the accusation of Russian meddling in the 2016 US presidential election. This has over shadowed other issues. This is evident from the fact that hell-bent on pursuing this issue, on July 13 only three days before the Helsinki summit there was indictment of 12 Russian military intelligence officers for allegedly hacking and releasing thousands of documents and e-mails that were damaging to US President Donald Trump's Democratic opponent, Hillary Clinton. Even though he had repeatedly denied Russia's involvement, and hence was not expecting such a development at this critical moment, Trump frankly tweeted, referring to US special prosecutor Robert Mueller's probe as foolishness and stupidity and now, the "Rigged Witch Hunt!".

It is important to note that the Russian Foreign Ministry, which has rejected the charges in the indictments, was also candid in stating that the intent of US Special Counsel Robert Mueller in levelling the charges almost on the eve of the Helsinki Summit could be to "spoil the atmosphere" for talks. This issue had been raised earlier and Russia had officially informed that it was ready to cooperate in investigating the matter. At the Helsinki summit Putin was asked whether he would extradite to the United States 12 Russian military intelligence officers recently indicted on charges of interfering in the US election. Being a shrewd political leader, Putin described the men as "alleged intelligence officers" and he launched into a long explanation of a 1999 treaty on Mutual Assistance on Criminal Cases, saying Moscow would be happy to question the men for US officials and even to allow those officials to be present at the questioning.

American Response

From the American perspective the outcome of Helsinki Summit is far from satisfactory. In fact, there have been strong and highly negative responses to the summit by political leaders and analysts in the USA and West. The American media is highly critical of Trump which is evident from the report in the *Washington Post* on July 17 which wrote a piece with the headline "Disgraceful, Shameful: Trump's defence of Putin." It is rather unexpected and most worrisome for Trump that some Republican Party members have joined Democrats in criticising him. For instance, Mitt Romney, the 2012 Republican candidate for President, called Trump's behaviour "disgraceful and detrimental to our democratic principles" and said it "undermines our national integrity and impairs our global credibility". Similarly, former Republican House Speaker Newt Gingrich, who in the past had defended Trump against criticism by more conventional Republicans, called the summit "the most serious mistake" of Trump's presidency—and one that "must be corrected—immediately." The most scathing remark has been made by Senator John McCain, the 2008 Republican presidential candidate and current Chairman of the Senate's Armed Services Committee. He has been critical of Trump and was against the summit itself. Hence he is candid in stating that Trump's press conference at the Helsinki Summit with Putin "was one of the most disgraceful performances by any President and a tragic mistake".

Thus, Trump has been met with a tidal wave of criticism from friends and critics alike after his summit with Russian President Vladimir Putin. Radio Free Europe reported that, as opined by analysts, Trump's embrace of Putin while belittling US agencies and allies was a betrayal of what the United States stands for.

Keir Giles, a Russia expert in Chatham House in London, has opined that Trump has discredited in his own country when faced with Putin at the summit. In fact, many analysts expected that Trump would raise issues concerning America such as Russia's interference in the US elections, Russia's annexation of Crimea, Russia's involvement in Eastern Ukraine etc. But none of them were mentioned in the press conference at the end of summit. Instead Trump made a scathing remark on his own country. According Mike Carpenter, a former Russia official with the White House National Security Council and a foreign policy adviser to Vice President Joe Biden, "The losers are US national security interests and the winner is Putin and the Kremlin regime that he represents". Expert on Russia Pomeranz has opined: "President Trump again showed an unwillingness to confront Russia about the interference with the 2016 election."

All these indicate that there will be a major challenge for Trump's presidency and his administration in the near future.

But being a smart politician Trump has often changed his stance and statements. This is evident again. For instance, as reported by AP, AFP and Reuters on the July 17 Trump said he accepts the US intelligence community's conclusion that Russia meddled in the 2016 US presidential election in his favour. However, he asserted that Russian actions did not have any impact on the outcome of the vote and his election. Moreover, he also backtracked from his remarks in Helsinki that he saw no reason to think that Russia had meddled, claiming on July 17 that he'd meant to say he saw "no reason why it would not be Russia" that had interfered in the election. He also reiterated that he had full faith and support for US intelligence agencies and on July 17 said his administration will move aggressively to repel any effort to interfere in the 2018 elections for US legislative posts. It is to be seen whether these statements will pacify his critics. Thus, Trump has been grudgingly apologetic to what he stated at the Helsinki Summit. Moreover, to pacify his critics, on coming back to Washington on July 18 Trump has promised that "big results" will eventually come from his summit with Russian President Vladimir Putin.

Russia's Response and Perspective

Russia's perspective even before the summit and response are quite in contrast to that of America. Being pragmatic, Russia did not have high expectations of the summit which is evident from the fact that the Russian leaders, including the Russian Foreign Minister Sergei Lavrov, have consistently maintained that the summit would be "the first step" in overcoming a crisis in bilateral relations. In an interview with Russia's RT television shortly before the summit, Lavrov had set the goalposts for the meeting: "The ideal outcome would be to agree to engage all the channels [of communication] on all divisive issues and also on those issues where we can already usefully cooperate."

Therefore, immediately after the summit, when Lavrov was asked what he thought of the meeting, he said it was "better than super." On July 15, Andrei Kortunov, head of a Russian Foreign Ministry think-tank in Moscow, agreed that the talks enable Putin "to make his point that Russia is not isolated, that Russia is a great power, and to some extent that Russia can even claim equal status with the United States, at least in the security field."

It is worth noting the observations made in the Russian media. In comments to Russian paper *Izvestiya,* Kosachyov was more specific about the bilateral agenda moving forward, emphasising Helsinki developments that barely attracted notice in the West. Russian expert Robert Coalson has stated on July 17 that subsequent to the summit, Russian political analyst Venediktov concluded that the delegations showed that the main US concerns at Helsinki were strategic security and the election interference, while Putin's concerns were Syria and "public relations". That showed that there were differences in the focus at the summit. At the same time it was a good beginning for both the countries. Thus, as opined by Coalson, "Russian Analysts see Helsinki Meeting 'As Opening To Normalisation'". In fact, this confirms what Russian leaders wanted and stated even before the summit. On the issue of 'Ukraine', Putin was frank in stating without challenge that it was Kyiv that was to blame for not implementing the Minsk peace accords, not Russia, as stated by Will Pomeranz, Deputy Director of the Kennan Institute for Advanced Russian Studies at the Wilson Center in Washington. Hence Putin was candid in not accepting any blame and instead accusing Ukraine for not implementing the Minsk peace accord. Thus, according to many Western commentators, the summit was a success for Putin and that Trump yielded to Putin.

At the same time Russia is happy since many analysts have opined that the outcome of the summit was in favour of Putin. At the same time even as the Helsinki summit was an advantage for Putin, under the prevailing scenario of responses in America, Russia may have to wait for words to be translated into action by Trump's administration for improving bilateral relations. In fact, under the prevailing pressure and criticism in America, it will be difficult to state how soon Putin and Trump will succeed in their objectives.

14

Russia's 'Vostok 2018' Military Exercises—Putin's Show Of Strength?

On August 28, 2018 the Russian Government announced that the 'Vostok-2018' (East-2018) military exercises will be carried out from September 11 to 15, 2018. These exercises will be held in Russia's Central and Eastern Military districts, in southern Siberia and the Far East. In fact, this will be a major military drill to take place in Russia since 1981. This was corroborated by Russia's Defence Minister Sergei Shoigu who declared that this would be the biggest military exercises in almost 40 years. In fact, he was referring to the military exercises that year (1981), which involved the Soviet and other Warsaw Pact forces and were the largest war drills ever carried out by the Soviet Union and its allies. In justification of his statement Sergei Shoigu mentioned that 'Vostok 2018' will involve almost 300,000 troops, more than 1000 aircraft; both the Pacific and Northern Fleets, and all Russian airborne units. More important is that 'Vostok -2018' has great geo-political and geo-strategic significance in view of the fact that there will participation of Chinese and Mongolian military personnel.

Hence several questions arise as to what are the objectives for carrying out this exercise, what is the cost for the country, whether this is a show of strength for the Russian President, Vladimir Putin, and so on. Perhaps from Russia's national interest there is a need for this military exercise. Firstly, although there is no super power rivalry between Russia and the West in contrast to what prevailed during the Soviet era, as expressed by the Kremlin spokesman Dmitry Peskov, such war games are "essential" in the current international situation which, he opined, was "often aggressive and unfriendly toward our country."

Secondly, in recent years, Russia's military has stepped up the frequency and scope of its military exercises, reflecting the Kremlin's multiple focus on modernising its armed forces and its tactics. This is evident from the fact that Russia last held large-scale war games in September 2017 known as 'Zapad 2017' (West 2017), jointly with Belarus in regions bordering NATO countries in the Baltics. Thirdly, it is a matter of significance that this is not a secret event. In fact, NATO spokesman Dylan White confirmed that Russia had briefed the alliance, which planned to monitor them. At the same time he is candid in stating: "'Vostok-2018' demonstrates Russia's focus on exercising large-scale conflict. It fits into a pattern we have seen over some time: a more assertive Russia, significantly increasing its defence budget and its military presence." In fact both Russia and the NATO members have conducted a flurry of military drills near Russia's borders during the last few years. Hence Russia insists that it will be responding to a growing NATO threat.

Fourthly, the timing is important since relations between Moscow and the West have deteriorated to a post-Cold War low. From the Western perspective, tensions have increased due to Russia's alleged annexation of Crimea in 2014, its role in wars in Syria and eastern Ukraine, and its alleged election meddling in the United States in 2016 and in Europe.

Fifthly, there is an ongoing conflicting situation that prevails in Syria during the last few years where Russia supports the Syrian President, Bashar al-Assad, while the USA and West support his Opposition parties. Hence possibly to consolidate its position, as per reports, Russia decided to undertake a major naval exercise from September 1 to 8 in the Mediterranean Sea which might further aggravate tensions between Moscow and the West over the Syrian issue. As reported by the Russian Defence Ministry, this involved 25 warships, including a missile cruiser, and 30 aircraft. The objective of Syrian President Assad, who is confident of strong support of Russia, seems to prepare a major assault to regain control of the Idlib Province, a hotbed of terrorists, the last major stronghold of the Syrian Sunni rebels.

In fact, Assad has reason to be comfortable since the Kremlin spokesman, Dmitry Peskov, was candid in stating on August 30 that the difficult situation in Syria justified the planned Russian naval drills in the Mediterranean. But as expected, the United States, Britain, and France have repeated their warning to Assad. In fact, anticipating likely conflict in the region, the UN Secretary-General, Antonio Guterres, warned on August 29, 2018 "about the growing risks of a humanitarian catastrophe in the event of a full-scale military operation" in Idlib.

Lastly, during two decades of his leadership of Russia, Vladimir Putin has focused on the defence sector and its modernisation, a major centre-piece of his administration. When Putin got elected for the fourth term as the President in May 2018, some analysts opined that he would bring about changes in how Russia's defence-industrial sector is managed. This has become evident from Putin's decision of replacing officials in the Defence Ministry and, sacking several Generals during the last several months. He is aware of the rampant corruption; that has been one of the major problems facing the economy and defence sector.

It is highly commendable that notwithstanding bilateral differences as mentioned above, there is cooperation between Russia's Roskosmos and America's NASA in conducting experiments in space research. At present a six-member crew, four from the USA and two from Russia, are in the International Space Station, and they will complete the exercise and return to earth in December 2018.

In conducting the 'Vostok-2018' military exercise, the objective of the Russian President, Vladimir Putin, is to show-case that Russia has retained its strong military power. This is evident from the fact that while addressing Russia's Defence Chiefs a few months back, Putin reiterated that Russia's military can overpower any potential foe. Putin perhaps indicated that it (the military) will continue to get priority in terms of state explenditure.

But at the same time the reality is quite complex and far from satisfactory. It also raises questions as to the timing and relevance of this military exercise. As opined by experts in the Stockholm International Research Institute (SIPRI) in May 2018, the Russian defence sector has been facing problems of credit crunch, lagging technology, piled up defence projects and so on. The Russian economic condition is in a bad shape due to multiple factors such as low economic growth, economic sanctions by the USA and Western countries on Russia for its alleged annexation of Crimea, its role in wars in Syria and eastern Ukraine, and its alleged meddling in the United States election and Europe. This is further evident from the inability of the Russian Government to pay dues on time for workers of the FIFA World Cup, massive agitation by pensioners for raising title pension-age, poor healthcare system and so on. But perhaps these issues are of secondary relevance for asserting Russia's global status.

Section - III
India-Russia Economic Relations

15

India's Exports to Russia Complexities and Contradictions

In the context of the economic liberalisation taking place simultaneously in the two countries, the potential for expanding trade between India and Russia is very considerable. There are, however, a number of complexities and contradictions - among them, the multiplicity of trade channels, the lack of transparency in the release of debt repayment rupee funds through so-called tenders, the uncertainties and irrationalities of Russia's import regulations and tax structure and the activities of fly-by-night operators out to make quick profits - which come in the way of the growth of India-Russia trade relations on a sound basis.

Indo-Russian trade seems to be poised for substantial growth in 1995. The target trade turnover of Rs 5,000 crore set during the Indo-Russian Joint Commission meeting held in July between Pranab Mukerjce. India's minister for external relations, and Yuri Yarov, deputy prime minister of the Russian Federation, seems quite attainable - given the latest trend in trade performance. This is evident from the fact that during the April-June quarter Indo-Russian trade turnover was about Rs 1.505 crore which shows a nearly two-fold increase over the level of Rs 797 crore reached in the corresponding period in 1994. Furthermore, The Russian side had given an indication of importing in 1995, 30,000 tonnes of tea, 20,000 tonnes of tobacco, 10,000 tonnes of soya meal and $ 100 million worth of medicines. These four items form a special category for which the Russian government calls for tenders in Russia and for which a part of the yearly accumulations of debt repayment amount of Rs 3,000 crore will be used. Both Indian and Russian policymakers may feel satisfied with this improved performance in trade volume as compared to the steep decline in trade in 1992-93 to only Rs 1,700 crore consequent upon the disintegration of the USSR. But this should not lead to complacency on the two sides if the trade relations between India and Russia are to be developed on rational and normal commercial bastes from the viewpoint of the long-term benefit of both countries.

In fact, under the process of economic liberalisation that is taking place simultaneously in the two countries, there should be greater possibilities for expanding trade between the two countries. But there are several complexities and contradictions in fully exploiting India's potentialities for increasing exports to Russia.

A major complexity in exports to Russia is the multiplicity of trade channels. At present there are four identifiable routes or hannels, each with sub-routes, all operating simultaneously. They are (a) Debt Repayment Rupee Account (DRA); (b) Escrow Account; (c) Hard Currency Account; and (d) the unofficial or semi-legal trade channel.

Under DRA of Rs 3,000 crore per year, there are two sub-routes. Under the first sub-route there arc four commodities falling under special category as already mentioned above. For importing these commodities the Russian government makes some allocation of funds which are finally disbursed through lenders. There is another sub-route which is available for importing from India any other commodity with due permission from the Russian government, whereby a registered firm in Russia can procure rupee funds after paying the equivalent amount of roubles through designated Russian agencies or banks. For getting access to rupee funds from Russian banks under DRA, any registered firm in Russia has to deposit upfront money of 30 percent in roubles in eight days and the rest of amount in 60-90 days or provide rouble cover by a bank guarantee. Hence there seems to be some advantage for the four commodities under the special category since the Russian government makes some budgetary allocation to the respective ministries for imports from India which is in a sense similar to the system which had prevailed under the

Soviet regime. But even for this, rouble payment is required. Upfront money is to be paid to a Russian bank which has procured rupee funds from Foreign Economic Bank of Russia known as VEB.

A great advantage for the use of DRA account is that rupee funds are offered at a discount of 20-30 percent (known in Russian parlance as a coefficient of about 0.7 percent which is reminiscent of the Soviet past when all foreign currencies were calculated in roubles at varying coefficients which was different from the so-called official exchange rates reflecting shadow value of rouble). For instance, officially \$ 1=4,500 roubles. But a Russian firm has to depos it about 3,550 roubles for getting the equivalent of \$ 1 for importing goods from India. In other words, one can get Rs 38-41 per US dollar against official exchange rate of Rs 31-32. This difference makes imports from India profitable. But this also amounts to devaluing the Indian rupee in the Russian market. Thirty percent discount is given if payment is made in 60 days and 20 percent discount for 90 days.

It appears that many trading firms prefer to pay upfront money in cash since bank credit and guarantee are available at very high interest rates of 5-10 percent per month. The payment of such high interest cuts the profit margin for the trading firm. Hence in many cases arrangements are made in advance and deals are finalised by trading firms so that letters of credit are opened by Russian importing agencies when goods are being shipped so that time for delivery is reduced and transaction completed within the stipulated period. But this involves a lot of problems and risks.

The second channel is Escrow account. India can port goods to Russia under the Escrow account funds held by a Russian enterprise or organisation which has accumulated these funds against previous exports to India. For instance, these are mainly defence-related units such as Aviaexport which supplied defence equipment to India in the past, the receipts of which were kept in Escrow account. An Escrow account may be operated in dollars or in rupees depending upon the nature of funds held by the Russian organisation. The rupee Escrow account was more prominent in the past and will be significant for some more time. But dollar Escrow account is gaining importance. The use of these funds depends upon the concerned organisations and there seems to be substantial freedom and flexibility in terms of the items to be imported into Russia or the destination of supplies, etc.

The third channel is the hard currency trade account for which there are hardly any restrictions for exports to Russia. Lastly, the unofficial or partly legal trade channel is a new phenomenon after the Soviet disintegration. This form of trade is carried out mainly by 'fly-by-night' operators from India and also by 'shuttlers' (known as 'Chclnochniki' in Russian) from the Russian side.

It is interesting to note that exports of certain goods such as tea or medicines may go simultaneously through more than one route or channel by same or different agencies which adds to the complexity of trading with Russia.

There is a general opinion among the officials in Russia and India that it may not be possible to know the precise volume of Indo-Russian trade. This means that the available data on trade may not reflect the actual volume of trade not only due to the multiplicity of trade channels including the semi-legal channel but also due to the fact that some trade may take place through non-Russian ports such as Nikalaevsk in Ukraine with the goods actually reaching Russia. According to one banking expert in Russia, the share of hard currency exports could be about 5-7 percent, while the shares of trade through debt repayment and Escrow account might be nearly equal, i.e., about 40 percent each. The quantum of unofficial or semi-legal trade is highly uncertain and hence speculative, but it is flourishing under prevailing conditions in both the countries.

As stated by one authentic source, under the debt repayment account, the Central Bank of Russia (CBR) releases rupee funds for imports as and when required to supplement the federal budgetary needs. Hence there is no regularity and certainty as to when and for what amount tenders will be issued. This is in contrast to the Soviet past when the amount or quantity of import was predetermined by the two governments in advance.

Moreover, there is lack of transparency in the release of rupee allocation for import of even special category goods since only designated Russian banks participate in the tender. Hence so far there is no effective and transparent mechanism for use of rupee funds. Bannerjee of Ranbaxy Lab's office in Moscow stated in this context that every Indian pharmaceutical firm is kept guessing as to which Russian organisation has got the rupee allocation from the Russian government so that upfront rouble cover is not required. The fact is that many ministries are involved—ministry of finance, ministry of health and ministry of foreign economic relations. Contacting Russian agencies with all uncertainties has become a task and hence many backdoor dealings with kickbacks, etc, continue which affect healthy competition. He further observed that exports through debt repayment channel is more profitable and the volume of orders is large.

Besides this, there are other hassles affecting India's exports of specific products such as pharmaceutical items to Russia. The registration of medicines for imports into Russia takes about five-six months so far as India is concerned, whereas for the US it takes only one or two weeks. Moreover, since 1994, for medicines originating from the Asian continent (India being the main country) every lot of Imports in Russia has to undergo random checking in Russian laboratories, whereas there is no need for quality checking for medicines imported from the US and even European countries are exempt from this checking. These conditions add to the cost and delays in India's exports of medicines to Russia.

Russian banks, a majority of which are single branch banks, are far from being developed and hence not able to handle various foreign trade operations. In fact, Russia's banking sector is undergoing crisis since many of them carry out speculative and unhealthy banking practices and there is lack of strict implementation of control by the CBR. One Moscow-based Indian trading firms had deposited the money with a Russian bank for payment for imports from India. This bank was closed down due to bankruptcy in the last week of August 1995 in the wake of the Russian government policy of extending the period of 'corridor' for exchange rate of rouble to the dollar.

One of the factors that has added to the complexity in India's exports to Russia is the irrationality in certain custom and import regulations. As stated by Umapati, president of a trading firm dealing in import of Indian goods, there were instances when the Russian authorities insisted on applying revised rates of value added tax (VAT) even for the transactions which were already finalised and settled and for which shipments were already made on the basis of the then prevailing VAT rate. This affected the deal and cut down earning. There was also a specific case in 1994 when one consignment of goods was imported from India and for which all duties and taxes including VAT were paid and they were kept in the godown in Moscow. After a few months when these goods were to be sold to a Russian organisation, it was insisted that VAT was to be paid again (despite showing the proof of payment of VAT) and, if necessary, an application could be made for refund. It appears that getting refund in Russia is a near impossibility.

In Russia taxes on imports are very high and tax laws and regulations are complicated and are changed very frequently. It appears that there are also several irrationalities in the prevailing tax and duty structure. For instance, it is cheaper to import readily packed tea in small packs from India ready for sale rather than import tea in bulk and get it processed and packed in Russia. This may be one of the reasons why the Tata joint venture project in tea in Russia could not take off. It was also pointed out by the representative of a Dubai-based shipping and clearing firm operating in Russia that import duties are charge in Russia on the weight of goods rather than on value of goods. Under the circumstances those who can manage to import goods by avoiding or bypassing payment of all taxes through bribery, etc, are benefited. Now there has been a realisation of these irrationalities and efforts are being made for introducing tax reforms. But this may take several months if not years.

It is ironical that although India was a major-supplier of certain traditional goods such as tea to the former USSR and Indian goods were well known in Russia, the image of Indian goods has been sagging in the Russian market. As observed by an Indian trade representative in Moscow, during the last two-three years non-specialists have entered the Russian market even for specialised products such as medicines. Some of them are also 'brief-case-traders' who are prepared to deal in any product since they do not have any long-term interest in cultivating the Russian market. They join hands with unscrupulous and often fake firms in Russia for making instant and maximum profit by selling goods disregarding quality or standards! The image of India in Russia is also being damaged by 'shuttiers' from Moscow who buy cheap and substandard goods in India and sell them at high prices back in their country. Considerable damage is being done by these elements. In the interest of promoting sound commercial relations between India and Russia, there is an urgent need for undertaking effective measures by policymakers in both countries to control this damage caused to India's exports to Russia.

One of the contradictions in Indo-Russian trade is that although the Soviet Union has disintegrated, some of the former network of importing organisations of the Soviet era continue. For instance, there are about 25 organisations such as Machinoexport, Energomash, Sovelektro, Rosvneshtrog, Legprom, etc, which are directly nominated by the Russian government for whom 'quota' is given for use of debt repayment rupee resources. They, however, get what is known as 'tselevie dengi' (object-oriented money) for importing specific goods from India. They act as specialised intermediate organisations for arranging imports and they carry names very much resembling the monopoly state agencies of the Soviet past. They, however, do not possess any funds themselves, but can only negotiate on behalf of the final buyers in Russia. Actual funds are available with these organisations or enterprises which are required to pay upfront money to a Russian bank out of their budget funds or provide for corresponding bank guarantees. It appears that some of these intermediate organisations continue to act in a monopolistic fashion and try to get maximum cuts and kickbacks for their services which possibly increases the cost of Indian goods to the Russian buyer.

In general most of the Russian enterprises organisations are facing financial constraints and although they may be in need of goods some of which India can offer, they are unable to provide upfront money and wait for two-three months for the delivery of goods. Therefore, Indian trading firms are at times expected to provide upfront money which is an added risk and uncertainty for them to get back their payment in the final analysis.

Another major contradiction is that in the post-Soviet scenario when a large number of private firms from foreign countries such as Siemens, Panasonic, Daewoo, Philips and so on have entered the Russian market for exporting their products and for establishing joint ventures in Russia, some Indian firms which had set up their representative offices in Moscow in the past are withdrawing from Russia. It is reliably learnt that HMT has closed its office in Moscow and Tata Tea has discontinued its joint venture project for a tea processing and packaging unit in Russia. Some of the engineering firms such as Thermax and Bharat Forge are making all efforts to survive and carry on their business in Russia against all odds. The position of relatively smaller firms dealing in garments and knitwear is no different despite the fact that they have been trading with Russia (and the former Soviet Union) for the last several years.

The seriousness of this issue lies in the fact that in the past, capacities were created in India for producing many of these products - consumer goods, machinery and equipment, pharmaceutical products and so on - for meeting the needs of the former Soviet market. At present the policy-makers in the countries do not seem to be much concerned about them. In this regard the selection of only four items for special allocation for use of debt repayment funds seems to be highly unsatisfactory. The selection seems to be based more on political considerations than on economic interests and realities in both the countries. For instance, the inclusion of tobacco has so far hardly served the purpose. In 1994-95, India's export of tobacco was only Rs 15 crore, which was just about 1.5 percent of total exports from India to Russia. The amount of $ 100 mn earmarked for import of medicines from India is far too low as compared to the volume of imports in the past.. Despite being pricewise competitive, Indian pharmaceutical firms have to struggle hard to export to Russia due to several other constraints.

It appears that there is demand for certain items of machinery and equipment such as boilers, forging equipment, crankshafts, etc, by Russian enterprises. If debt repayment rupee credits are made available to them as in the past, Indus exports of such items may increase significantly for the benefit of Russian enterprises.

Hence there is need for reconsideration of the issue by the policy-makers in both the four countries and the solution should be based on the long-term economic interests of both the countries. One possible solution could be recasting the list for budgetary allocation by incorporating all major items which were important in the export list from India to the former Soviet Union in 1991. The Russian government should also facilitate use of rupee credits for importing goods from India by adopting a more flexible policy, for instance, by not insisting on the payment of upfront money to the CBR.

Both Indian and Russian governments have agreed to consider joint venture proposals for which part of the Rs 3,000 crore of debt repayment funds could be utilised. In this regard there is an urgent need to set up an Indo-Russian joint venture in the banking and finance sector to promote mutual trade and joint industrial ventures in both the countries. While the State Bank of India has got its office in Moscow, its activities are confined mainly to settlements and not commercial transactions. It was reported in the Indian press that Canara Bank was to open a branch in St Petersburg. The EXIM Bank of India evinced interest in promoting India's trade with Russia and other CIS and east European countries. Serious efforts should be made jointly by some of these Indian banking institutions to set up a joint Indo-Russian bank. To build up initial capital Indian banks should consider buying up Rs 1,000 crore per year for a period of five to seven years from the Russian government (Central Bank of Russia) out of the debt repayment rupee funds held by Russia by paying equivalent amount in dollars (or roubles) at a discount of about 40 per cent, i.e., paying Rs 45-50 per dollar. The Russian government is already offering discount of 30 percent to traders. The Russian partner organisation in this banking joint venture could put up its contribution to the initial capital so that this bank can function on a purely commercial basis with due approval and permission of both the governments. Genuine exporters on both sides can benefit from such a banking institution. It appears Vietnam has already set up a joint venture bank in Russia with a view to promoting economic relations between the two countries. Hence this proposal seems to be viable.

In conclusion, it may be observed that India's exports to Russia seem to be picking up after a sharp decline in 1992-93. This improvement in trade performance could be partly attributed to the efforts made by governments in both the countries during the last two years.

However, there should be no room for complacency since there are many complexities and contradictions which seem to effect the promotion of Indo-Russian trade relations on a rational basis. They are multiplicity of trade channels, lack of transparency in the release of debt repayment rupee funds through 'tenders', uncertainties and irrationalities in Russia's import regulations and tax structure, its underdeveloped banking sector, lack of specialised Indian agencies for exporting specialised products to Russia, withdrawal of established Indian firms and agencies from Moscow after the Soviet disintegration, and the activities of emerging unscrupulous elements out to make quick profits rather than cultivate the Russian market with long-term interest.

These complexities need to be resolved for further promoting trade and economic relations between India and Russia. It is necessary to reconsider the list of goods for export from India for which special allocation is being made from the debt repayment funds. There is need for introducing transparency in the release of debt repayment funds. Irrationalities in Russia's tax and duty structures may be eliminated through the proposed tax reforms. Considering the potentialities of the huge Russian market, India's leading companies should give due importance to this country for promoting trade and joint ventures. This may also help in boosting India's image in Russia. In this regard India and Russia should consider setting up a joint venture in banking and finance for promoting Indo-Russian economic relations for which a part of the debt repayment funds could be utilised.

16

India-Russia Economic Relations: Challenges and Opportunities

The visit of the Russian president Vladimir Putin to India in October 2000 assumes great significance in strengthening and promoting wide ranging relations between India and Russia. The leaders of both the countries have signed a Declaration of strategic partnership and have agreed to work together on various international issues to build a multi-polar world, while strengthening bilateral co-operation in defence and military-technical matters. So far as defence relations are concerned, India has agreed to buy over $3 billion worth of arms from Russia covering a wide range of defence equipments such as 310 T-90 tanks, MiGs, aircraft carrier Admiral Gorshkov, 18 Smerch multiple rocket launchers (MRLs), lease of 4 Tu22 Backfire bombers etc. All these equipments will enable India to strengthen defence capability of all the concerned wings — army, navy and air-force. It is significant that the Su-30 agreement incorporates joint production, joint marketing and buyback of equipment manufactured in India's HAL. It is hoped that the provisions of this agreement are realised for the benefit of both India and Russia in the foreseeable future. So far as Russia is concerned, in the immediate future Putin has ensured that his country's interest is well taken care of even as India has lately tried to diversify its market for arms purchases looking to Europe and Israel. Needless to add that India being a major buyer of Russian defence equipments, this agreement will assure Russia's Military Industrial Complex (MIC) that it can depend upon India to earn much needed hard currency.

It is observed that this declaration is aimed at taking India-Russia ties to an 'even higher qualitatively new level'. That India and Russia (successor to the former Soviet Union) have always maintained good political relations, this declaration reaffirms the friendly and historic ties between the two countries. However, what is significant and crucial is that in the declaration, there is specific mention that both the countries will cooperate to fight against international terrorism, separatism, organised crime and trafficking in narcotics. This assumes importance in the present context when both the countries are threatened by these evil forces. There is thus substantial commonality of views between India and Russia on several international issues.

Apart from the declaration of strategic partnership, there are nine agreements signed covering co-operation in the fields of science and technology, banking, agriculture, joint exploration of natural gas and so on. In a way most of these agreements reflect continuity of co-operation in several areas including nuclear research for peaceful purposes. The Russian president has succeeded in concluding agreement with Indian leaders on the supply of Russian equipments to the much publicised and widely debated Kudan Kulam Nuclear power plant being built in South India.

So far as India is concerned, the visit of Putin should assume importance because in the sphere of trade and economic relations between the two countries much is required to be done. After the Soviet break-up, Russia has been passing through the period of transition from the former socialist system to a market oriented economy. This transition has been difficult and painful for Russia and the process is not complete. Over these years, Russia has been suffering from lack of economic stability, overall economic decline, problems of restructuring of production, problems of ownership arising from 'mass privatisation', social consequences of political and economic reforms resulting in unemployment, corruption, economic crime and decline in the standard of living of a large section of the population and so on.

Impact of Economic Reforms in Russia on Trade with India

Many of these problems that Russia has been facing in its economic sphere have affected India's trade and economic relations with Russia. For instance, as per the DGCI and S data, total trade turnover between India and Russia declined sharply from over $ 2,368 million in 1991-92 to $ 860 million in 1992-93. Although there was some improvement in trade turnover in subsequent years, during the period 1993-1999, India's exports to Russia have been in the range of about $ 600 to 1,000 million per annum. Annual export data does not show any steadiness and in fact there have been wide fluctuations in exports over the years. Similarly, India's yearly imports from Russia have been fluctuating in the range of $ 250 to $ 850 million. For India, the former Soviet Union was an important trading partner of India, which is no more the case at present. Similarly, India has lost its position among Russia's foreign trade partners. Moreover, there is lack of growth and dynamism which should be a matter of concern for the policy-makers and business community at large.

It is important to note that some large industrial houses which were operating for many years during the Soviet era wound up their establishments in Moscow presumably due to uncertain and unfavourable socio-economic conditions prevailing in the country. Equally significant was the fact that several projects that were initiated in the early 1990's by some reputed Indian companies to set up processing units in Russia including that of Tata's tea processing and packaging unit miserably failed. India's finance minister Yashwant Sinha has, in his address in Mumbai during Putin's meeting with Indian business community, opined that there were a few shortcomings with regard to trade with Russia. There are some experts and businessmen who consider that the prevailing mechanism of trade has not done much good for promoting India-Russian trade. What is more, 80-85 percent of this annual export trade is accounted for by debt repayment funds (DRF) and that too mainly concentrated on a few traditional items such as tea, coffee, tobacco, rice, leather etc. There are very few non-traditional items in India's export basket with the exception of pharmaceutical products. Hence one would legitimately question about the prospects of India's trade with Russia beyond say, 2005 when DRF are fully utilised. Hence the visit of Russian president Vladimir Putin's to India and agreements signed by both the countries and opportunities created after the visit should be utilised for finding ways and means to revive trade and economic relations between India and Russia.

Notwithstanding the prevailing situation as mentioned above, there has been a realisation on the part of both in India and Russia about vast potential for growth in trade economic relations between the two countries given their large size, vast resource potentialities, skilled manpower etc. Both the countries have also good record of trade and economic co-operation during the Soviet era. Moreover, as pointed out by India's finance minister at the Mumbai meeting with the Russian president, both the countries have initiated economic policies of liberalisation, privatisation and greater integration with the world economies which should enhance scope for closer economic ties. Hence as an appropriate step in this direction leading Indian business groups such as the CII, FICCI have rightly taken initiative in identifying some specific areas of cooperation with Russia.

For example, in their assessment, given skilled manpower from India and Russia's strong R and D base coupled with hardware design capabilities, there is vast scope for the two countries to collaborate in areas such as IT including advanced computing, biotech (including pharmaceuticals), telecommunication, training of personnel in managerial and financial services and so on. There are other areas of co-operation which are identified by Russia and were specified during the recent visit of the Russian deputy prime minister Ilya Klebanov to India. They include power engineering, new materials, utilisation of industrial waste, environmental control systems and instrumentation.

Putin's Claim of Qualitative Improvement in Russian Economy

Vladimir Putin's visit to India and in particular to Mumbai, the financial capital of India and his meeting organised by the CII and FICCI to discuss "India Russia Economic Co-operation" in which 350 CEOs of leading industrial firms of India interacted with the Russian president, assume great significance. As the long awaited visit of the Russian president to India has materialised, he has tried to convey to the Indian business circles that there has been a qualitative change in politico-economic life in Russia. So far as Russian economy is concerned, Putin seems to have turned the corner after the country experienced major economic crisis resulting from Rouble devaluation in August 1998. This is evident from the performance of the economy during the year 2000. The GDP growth for the year 2000 as a whole is expected to be about six to seven percent. Industrial output has registered a record 10 percent growth during the period January-August 2000 against the corresponding period of the last year. On the agricultural front, grain collection has exceeded 70 million tons which is about 10 million tons more than that in 1999. This will reduce the dependence of Russia on the import of food grains. So far as the foreign trade sector is concerned, as of 1-8-2000, Russia has achieved a trade surplus of $38 billion as against $20 billion in the previous year by trading mainly with countries outside the CIS. What should be equally gratifying to Putin is that gold and foreign exchange reserves have exceeded $24 billion in August 2000 as against $13 billion when he formally took office in January 2000. Inflation has been brought down to below 40 percent and exchange rate of rouble has been stable at around roubles 26-27 to a dollar.

Continuing the record of good performance, according to available official sources, Russia's tax collection has exceeded by about 75 percent to reach 53 billion roubles ($2 billion by August 2000) and that profits of about 51,800 large and medium firms have risen by 110 percent during January-July 2000 over the level of the corresponding period of last year. Sector-wise, the pre-tax profit making units were—communication, tourism, food processing, and wholesale trade of industrial products. In the opinion of some analysts, Russia's improved financial position is partly due to rise in world prices of oil and natural gas. It is estimated that at the minimum international price of $24 per barrel, there will be additional revenue to the tune of 54-60 billion Roubles (about $2 billion) to the Federal budget. Hence it is contended that the Russian economy may be vulnerable if there is decline in world energy prices. Notwithstanding this, there is overwhelming view in Russia that there is definite improvement in Russia's economic performance during the year 2000. Emphasising Russia's economic performance, Putin has called upon Indian entrepreneurs to make use of opportunities now available in Russia.

With this improvement in Russia's economy, there should be favourable influence on the general standard of living in the country. Hence there are expectations of increase in domestic demand for a wide range of consumer goods. In that case import demand for several consumer goods may go up. This situation may open up possibilities for India to step up exports of both traditional items such as tea, coffee, readymade garments, medicines and even consumer durables. However, in view of the fact that at present most of these traditional items are exported against the DRF, the Russian government should be persuaded to auction rupee funds with greater regularity and transparency. This may create better opportunity and incentive and even provide a good basis for reliable and large export houses from India to supply good quality products to the Russian market.

Western Assessment of Russian Economic Scene

On the claims and statements made by the Russian leaders on the economic situation in their country, it may be worthwhile to consider the assessment of the premier international financial institutions. For instance, in the assessment of the IMF experts, Russian economy has shown positive signs of development. Michael Mussa, the IMF research Director has observed 'after years of dithering and delay, important areas of structural reforms are beginning to move forward in Russia' (Radio Free Europe/Radio Liberty Report of 28-9-2000). In fact, in early 2000, the IMF experts had made a forecast of only about 1.5 percent annual GDP growth for Russia. But after observing improved economic performance, the forecast has been revised to seven percent. However, it is further opined that Russia should take advantage of current favourable economic conditions to boost its structural reforms and that the IMF would assist Russia 'only if unforeseen difficulties arose'. On Russian economy the IMF Moscow representative Martin Gilman has also opined (RFE/RL 20/9/2000) that the Russian government's budget policy is sound and plays a positive role in laying the foundation for macro economic stability which will enable the country to speed up reform process in the medium term.

It is important to note that the IMF assessment is further collaborated by the World Bank which has also been impressed with the economic programme of Putin's administration. The vice president of the World Bank Johannes Linn stated on 23rd September 2000 at the IMF-World Bank meeting held in Prague that the World Bank could agree for a loan of US$ 1.1 billion provided Russia implements legislation to improve shareholders right in privatised units.

A further evidence of the recognition of improvement of the Russian economy is that in September 2000 the international bank rating agency 'Thomson Bank Watch' has upgraded Russia's debt rating from CCC to B. In its assessment Russia has performed well in its 'fiscal and external sector positions' and has achieved greater political stability. As a result there is increase in domestic demand which is a positive sign of economic growth. This improved rating is significant because in the year 2001 Russia is expected to borrow about $ 5 billion abroad as visualised in the draft budget of the Russian Federation submitted to the Duma on 29th August 2000.

From the above account it is evident that the assessment of international financial institutions is definitely positive so far current Russian economic performance is concerned. However, both the IMF and World Bank have put some conditions such as speeding up of economic restructuring, ensuring ownership rights in privatised units to ensure that Russia stays on course of reform process of its economy. In this regard, some western analysts opine that lack of transparency in the holding and transfer of ownership shares in corporate firms, disputes over minority shareholders and their rights, persisting lawlessness continue to affect development of a truly market economy. In short, the Russian leaders have to still to go a long way to improve economic conditions in the country.

Unresolved Economic Issues

There are several problems and issues which still confront the policy-makers and they should be analysed and considered objectively. Firstly, M-L Factor has assumed great importance. (In the former Soviet Union M-L meant Marxism-Leninism and now in Russia M-L stands for

Money- Laundering). Money laundering has become a major problem since millions of dollars are being continuously siphoned off from the country by semi-legal and illegal means. According to available reports, over the last one decade, the quantum of money being laundered from the country every year has been more than what the country has received from various international financial institutions. But the irony of the matter is that on the issue of money laundering the Russian policy-makers do not appear to have paid much attention and presumably therefore have not achieved much success so far. But M-L issue has often caused much criticism and embarrassment to Russia's policy makers. In an effort to tackle the problem of money laundering although Russia has signed the convention in May 1999, the same has not been ratified even by September 2000 presumably due to bureaucratic and technical hurdles. The Russian government has, therefore, now urged Putin to submit the same to the Duma (the Russian parliament) for ratification. At a time when Russia badly needs resources for development, outflow of hard currency from the country on a large scale adversely affects the economy and sends unfavourable signals abroad. The issue of money laundering is also linked with the pervasive problem of mafia and other related economic crimes in Russia which are affecting economic development in the country.

Secondly, Russia has a major problem of repayment of foreign debt which is exceeding $ 150 billion, although part of this debt is being carried forward from the Soviet era. While Russia has not defaulted on debt repayment, it has managed to reschedule its debt to the London Club. In the year 2001, Russia has to pay foreign debt of US$ 14.5 billion, but in the budget for the next year provision has been made for only US$ 11.3 billion. Hence Russia has to mobilise additional resources for repayment of debt which will exert pressure on the budget.

Thirdly, Russia has been facing the problem of wage arrears for the last several years affecting even crucial sectors of the economy such a coal mining, power generation etc. While the severity of the problem might have become less, the current wage arrears exceeds two billion roubles ($ 75-80 million) causing some burden on the Federal State budget.

Fourthly, the Russian government has not been able to put in place ownership rights even as the policy of large scale privatisation of state property has been carried out since the last eight to nine years. This is particularly affecting the interest of foreign investors. Similarly, the Russian government has been slow in carrying out the much needed tax reforms, since the present tax system is highly complex and open to misuse by the authorities to harass the genuine entrepreneurs. In this context the observation of the foreign minister of Japan seems relevant. He has opined that while Japan has given a loan of $6 billion to Russia, investing that amount has become impossible because "Russia's tax system, lack of transparency in concluding contracts and legal mechanisms do not promote formal economic cooperation".

Lastly, although Putin has been able to get the support of the Duma for of his policies, there are on-going conflicts between some oligarchs particularly, Gussinsky and Boris Berezovsky on the one hand and Russian government on the other. Similarly, some regional governors are unhappy with the consolidation of power back with the centre after Putin has assumed presidentship. While it may be too early to predict as to how these issues are likely to be resolved, they have potentiality to affect economic development in the country.

Hence if Putin will succeed in solving these issues and is able to push through necessary legislation and more importantly implement the policies, then Russia may very well succeed in creating proper investment climate to attract more investment opportunities from foreign countries. Hence Indian policy-makers and the business community should also watch closely developments in Russia's economic scene to draw necessary conclusions from India's own interest and perspective.

Putin's Economic Priorities

In fact, from the available Russian published sources, it appears that efforts are being made during the last few months to find necessary solutions to the problems facing the country. For instance, Putin has given priority to implement tax reforms by proposing to reduce the tax burden, to simplify the procedures and also simplify customs regime. Similarly, German Gref the minister in charge of Economic Development and Trade has announced in early September 2000 that 16 new pieces of legislation will be ready in two months bringing Russian laws into line with international standards and thus creating 'comfortable conditions' for investors. He has urged that Russia needs far more investment to consolidate present economic growth. This is important also because in the next one to two years Russia expects to become a member of the World Trade Organisation.

The policy to attract foreign capital is possibly in response to Putin's initiative and directives that Moscow must provide foreign investors more assistance both 'moral and organisational' to enable them to face challenges in dealing with the Russian market. This aspect has been reaffirmed by Putin during his meeting in Mumbai with Indian entrepreneurs inviting them to invest in the Russian economy. There is another important policy decision that the Russian government is seriously considering, that is the introduction of 'Revised Production Sharing Agreement'. This is necessary for Russia in order to attract foreign investment. According to the Russia's Deputy Energy minister Valerii Garipov, if this policy is introduced, then Russia can count on a much as $80 billion income over the next decade.

All these are policy initiatives undertaken during the last few months by the Putin's administration which are intended to attract foreign investment in Russia from several countries and there seems to be some success in this regard. For instance, on the 29th September 2000, when Putin met German Chancellor Gerhard Schroeder in Moscow, among other issues, the main point of their discussion was on the economy including promoting small and medium sized businesses in Russia and Putin seems to have got some positive-response from Germany. On 2nd October 2000, the European Bank for Reconstruction and Development (EBRD) has recapitalised loan of US$ 30 million to Russia's International Moscow Bank which is an indication of growing confidence of western banks in Russian economy. Putin has also solicited interest of Japanese leaders in Russia's economic development of the Far Eastern regions neighbouring Japan. But the Russian leaders should remedy the situation as observed by the Japanese foreign minister.

Need to Evolve Appropriate Trade Strategy for India

Thus, on the assumption that Russia under the leadership of Vladimir Putin will be able to invigorate the economy and solve at least major problems mentioned above, there can be a window of opportunity for India to promote and boost economic relations with Russia. But for achieving this it may be necessary for the Indian policy-makers and business community to work out appropriate strategy for promoting trade and economic co-operation with Russia. India has a pending debt of about $4 billion to be repaid in the next four to five years.

Moreover, with fresh defence purchases of $3 billion, the total debt burden will increase to more than $7 billion in the coming years. Hence if serious efforts are not made at present India will have to suffer persisting adverse trade balance with Russia. Therefore, it is in India's own interest to make all efforts to boost exports to Russia. In this context it is worth appreciating that against total trade turnover of $1.57 billion in 1999, a target of $5 billion has been set by the Indian business community. While this target seems to be rather ambitious but it not unachievable if an appropriate economic strategy is worked out and implemented.

But for achieving that target several serious efforts are to be made. Some points for consideration are the following:

1. There is urgent need for transparency and regularity in the utilisation of Debt Repayment funds by the Russian authorities. This would promote exports from India by established and reputed Indian firms on a competitive basis and this will be in the interest of both India and Russia to ensure supply of right quality products and maintaining punctuality of delivery schedules etc.
2. Against the traditional approach of promoting and emphasizing only on export trade, it is necessary that greater attention be given to promote economic activities pertaining to joint ventures and production sharing etc. Areas of activity identified by the CII and FICCI such as IT, Pharmaceuticals, diamond cutting etc. deserve particular attention.
3. There are other areas and branches such as exploration and exploitation of non-ferrous minerals, exploitation of forest

based products (including paper manufacturing), manufacture of consumer goods including textile fabrics and apparels, knitwear garments, food processing etc. in which India can be competitive in the Russian market and has an advantage. Similarly, in areas such as soft-wear sector, development of tourism etc. hold some promise and need to be explored for the mutual benefit of both India and Russia.

4. Needless to emphasise that due legal and financial guarantees be obtained from the Russian side both from appropriate Russian organisations and official bodies to ensure that joint ventures function without major obstacles.
5. Russian policy-makers are now giving greater emphasis on promoting small and medium enterprises in their country. India has a fairly good record of long experience in this regard which may be of some relevance for the development of enterprenurship skills in different regions in Russia. At the same time, it is desirable and even necessary that in the growing dynamic and promising Russian economic context, large and reputed Indian industrial houses which have withdrawn or shied away from the Russian market should take a fresh look and initiative in undertaking joint venturer and/ or production sharing activities to make a significant impact on India-Russia economic relations. A part of Debt Repayment Funds (DRF) can be utilised for promoting such joint ventures to be set up in Russia for which machinery and equipment can be exported from India. It will be worthwhile to create 'India-Russia Venture-Capital Fund' of say $ 5 billion for promoting joint ventures in Russia and India. The Governments of both India and Russia should contribute in creating such a fund. In fact, some part of the balance of the DRF can be earmarked for this purpose. In addition to these, banking and other financial institutions and the private sector organisations in India and Russia should also be associated in this regard both for creating such a fund and for managing it on sound business principles.

17

India-Russia Economic Ties: Trends, Constraints and Prospects

While there is continuity in close political relations between India and Russia after the Soviet break-up, trade and economic ties have badly suffered. India's exports to Russia have declined singnificantly albeit a modest upward swing during the last few years. India's exports of traditional items such as tea, coffee, textiles etc, in which India had a monopoly position in the Soviet era have been the worst affected being unable to meet competition in the Russian market. Only a few items such as pharmaceutical have shown rising trend.

Chaotic political and economic conditions, breakdown of old institutions and practices, role of mafia in the initial period, complexities of debt repayment system adversely affected India's export to Russia.

But Russia has been able to maintain exports to India which consist of ferrous and non-ferrous minerals, fertilizers, newsprint, power plants equipment etc.

Indian exporters to Russia face constraints such as high risk factor of the Russian market, 'information gap' about new Russian firms, high cost of transportation of goods etc.

However, initiatives have been taken by both the Indian and Russian government as also trading associations to promote trade and economic ties.

Hence three alternative scenarios can be visualised—Ambitious-optimistic Scenario under which trade turnover of $ 10 bn by 2010 and $ 20 bn by 2015 can be reached, if constraints are removed; Pessimistic Scenario of possible decline in trade turnover if constraints persist and Pragmatic Scenario if some major problems are solved with joint efforts of India and Russia at state and private sector levels.

During the Soviet era, which ended about 18 years ago, India enjoyed close and cordial relations with that country in all spheres, namely political, defence and economic. India and the former Soviet Union enjoyed preeminent positions in their mutual relationships. While both India and Russia have maintained and sustained strong political and defence ties, thereby ensuring continuity in relations between the two countries, that is not so in respect of trade and economic relations, particularly what concerns India's exports to Russia. There is no conflict of interest between the two countries; yet bilateral trade has been faltering. An efforts has been made here to examine some of the important issues of trade and economic relations such as general trends in bilateral trade; problems and constraints; policy initiatives and measures taken to remove the bottlenecks and prognosticate the future.

Trade and Trend Analysis

The Indo-Russian aggregate trade data during the last about 18 years for some benchmark years are given in Table 1 and data regarding India's exports to Russia for major commodity groups are given in Table 2. On the basis of aggregate India-Russia trade data published by the Centre for Monitoring the Indian Economy, the following important observations may be made. First, India's total exports to Russia declined by about 45 percent between 1991-92 and 2000-2001, which indicates that there was significant southward trend during the 1990s. In fact, this downswing persisted up to 2004-2005, when India's exports to Russia were at their nadir amounting to just $ 631 millions which meant that it was only 40 percent of the level on the eve of the Soviet break-up. Subsequently there was marginal increase in India's exports to Russia. According to the World Fact Book report Russia's total commodity imports in 2007 were about $ 260 billion, which meant that India's share was less than 0.5 percent, as compared to China's share of 9.7 percent in the Russian import market. It needs to be mentioned that in 1991 India's exports to Russia was higher than that of China. Hence India's export performance to Russia has been very poor and its share in the total import trade of Russia has been negligible.

Secondly, in contrast to this poor export performance, India's imports from Russia, albeit downswings in the 1990s, have increased spectacularly since 2000, and by 2007, it zoomed by three and half times. More importantly, there has been consistent, upswing trend over the years. This clearly shows that Russia has been able to sustain its exports to India. Thirdly, India-Russia total trade turnover passed through a decadal decline between 1991 and 2001. This trade slump was particularly evident in the last decade during which Russia faced severe political and economic crisis after the Soviet break-up. Hence trade data indicates high fluctuations over the years due to lack of stability in trade relations between the two countries. However, India-Russia total trade turnover in 2006-2007 showed modest increase over the level of 1991-1992. More significantly, it has more than doubled during the past seven years and this increase has been mainly due to sharp increase in Russia's exports to India. According to a FICCI report, India's total trade turnover with Russia in the fiscal year 2007 was about four billion dollars, growing by about nine percent since the previous fiscal year.

Finally, data about trade balance, i.e. exports minus imports gives some interesting picture. India had positive trade balance during the last decade as well as in 2000-2001. However, since 2003-2004 the situation has dramatically changed. India has negative trade balance with Russia that maintained a northward trend year after year. Moreover, this data exclude the value of India's imports of defence goods and equipments from Russia, which could be an additional \$1-2 billion. Thus, it appears India has to make net payment of more than \$ 2-3 billion per year to Russia. Hence this should be a matter of great concern for Indian policy-makers to bridge this gap. It is desirable that there should be proper balance between exports and imports; hence such a huge adverse trade balance is against India's economic interest.

On the basis of analyses of trends in trade by major commodity groups, it may be stated that major items of exports from India to Russia are drugs, pharmaceutical products, fine chemicals, and traditional items such as tea, coffee, readymade apparels. It is important to note that there was sharp decline in the case of traditional items between 2000 and 2007, which is evident from the data given in Table 2. From that data it is also evident that since the last seven years, India has been loosing its share in the Russian market with regard to important traditional items of export such as tea, coffee, readymade garments, cotton yarn etc. Only in the case of pharmaceutical products there was major increase in India's exports to Russia. While it is necessary to examine the reasons for this trend, it is equally necessary to find ways and means to increase India's exports of these commodities. In the case of these traditional items India had a monopoly position during the Soviet era. If is evident that after the Soviet break-up and under the transformed scenario of Russia's transition to market economy, Indian exporters could not maintain and sustain this monopoly position. This may be due to variety of reasons: complexities of utilisation of Debt Repayment Funds; multiplicity of payment channels; increasing role of 'shuttle traders' often resorting to unfair trading practices, trading in goods of substandard quality, dumping low quality goods to get quick profits; role of mafia elements from both the sides; economic crisis conditions prevailing in Russia in the 1990s; growing competition of Russian market during the last several years and so on.

Moreover, by 2005-2006 India had paid off major part of its Soviet era debt to Russia at the rate of about one billion dollars per year. Hence this lack of DRF might be partly contributing to this decline in India's exports to Russia. In the case of tea and coffee, other producers' such as Sri Lanka, China and Brazil seem to have entered the Russian market in a big way with specific brands to successfully capture the market. There was another setback for exports of several traditional items such as tea, coffee, rice and tobacco due to a notification issued by Russia's animal and plant health watchdog Rosselkhoznadzor, which banned import of these items from India with effect from 28 January 2008. India has urged the Russian authorities to lift this ban since sufficient steps have been taken to safeguard the health of consumers of these items. It is important to note that in the case of some items such as spices, cashew, rice etc, exports in the past were for the entire Soviet Union, meeting demand of different regions such as Central Asia, the Caucasus and the Baltic.

In contrast to the traditional items medicines, Pharmaceuticals and fine chemical items are the only major group which have maintained growth in exports to Russia from $ 109 million in 2000 $ 271 million in 2007, say nearly three-fold increase in seven years. In fact, this growth has somewhat arrested total decline in India's exports to Russia. India's leading pharmaceutical companies such as Dr Reddy's, Ranbaxy, GlenMark, Lupin etc have played an important rols in this regarde. India's exports to Russia includes medicines such as HIV drugs, anti-TB, diabetes medicines to fight against what are known as 'rich man's diseases' even as India also exports other medicines including cough syrups for which there is great demand in Russia. India's exports mainly comprise of generic products as against innovation branded products that Russia imports from Europe and the USA. It is important to note that India is competitive in Russian market for a wide range of medicines. In the opinion of some experts, Indian products are 50-60 percent cheaper than comparable items from Europe and hence it is advantageous for Russia to import from India.

India has scope and potentiality for increasing exports of pharmaceutical products to Russia. This is because Russian market is about $ 9 billion which is about two percent of world market, while at present India's share is only about three percent in Russia's market. As stated by Alexander Dmitriyev, Russia's leading producers of medicines have started producing medicines of generic character under original brands. It is worthwhile to remember that in 2005 some Russian companies have displayed a tendency towards mergers and takeovers. For instance, a Russian investor purchased five pharmaceutical enterprises owned earlier by the US company ICN. Now Pharmastandart holding company, is one of the leading firms in Russia. At the same time, considering huge market some foreign pharma companies such as Hungary's Gedepm Richtcrhave built factories in Russia. It is equally important to note that the Russian state has become more active in the pharma market to meet the needs of certain section of the population such as pensioners, invalids etc. in the country. According the Indian commerce minister, several Indian companies have been investing in Russia in diverse fields such as energy, IT, Pharma, telecom, manufacturing etc. For instance, India has invested over one billion dollars in Sakhalin 3 in India-Russia joint venture for exploration of oil in Siberia, which is one of the largest investments. Similarly, India's one of the largest software companies, Tata Consultancy Services or TCS has opened a representative office in Russia in March 2008. About a hundred Indian companies are registered in Russia, majority of which are trading companies. More importantly, some leading Indian pharma companies have also opened their establishments in Russia, which have made positive contributions to enhancing trade and economic ties between India and Russia. Even as there is wide scope for India, Indian pharma companies face some constraints in increasing their exports to Russia. For instance, it is pointed out by FICCI that while it takes two years for Indian companies to register generic pharmaceutical products in Russia, applications for registration made by European firms are normally cleared in a year. Hence it is opined "Indian pharma companies feel that if the dossiers submitted by them are as per guidelines, the Russian government should reduce the registration time to one year". In the opinion of some experts, regulatory mechanism could be modified in the case of well known Indian pharma companies which are famous beyond any doubt and have established Research and Development facilities. They produce medicines of international quality standards (Good Manufacturing Practice). Hence for such companies duration for registration can be further reduced for mutual benefit. In turn, India should also take strong measures so that there is no scope for unscrupulous exporters or firms, which have spoiled India's name and image in the past in the Russian market by exporting sub-standard drugs.

Russian Exports to India

Russia's major items of export to India are iron and steel products, fertilizer, non-ferrous metals, synthetic rubber and a host of other items, which account for about 50 percent of total exports. In 2007, India also imported wheat from Russia to the extent of $ 156 million. India imports significant quantities of newsprint, transport equipment, organic chemicals, project goods and so on. Besides exporting a wide range of goods, Russian top companies are eyeing the lucrative Indian market in sectors like construction, hotels, telecoms, civil nuclear cooperation and energy, which shows dynamic approach of Russia in the Indian market. In the background of decades of cooperation with India in the field of ferrous and non-ferrous metallurgy. Russian companies such as Rusal and Tyzapromexport have offered joint venture participation with India to produce titanium oxide in Olivia, and set up aluminum plants. Russian research centers and Steel Authority of India have established co-operation in the field of research for mutual benefit. Russia has been playing an important role in setting up power plants including the nuclear power plant at Kudankulam, which is helping India ensure her energy security. The changed scenario of cooperation has elevated the bilateral relations from largely a buyer-seller level to the plains of partnership, which will be beneficial for both countries.

Yet the whole gamut of relationships is not entirely devoid of problems. There are several constraints facing the Indian companies in exporting to Russia. First, there has been a perception among many Indian businessmen regarding the high risk factor with regard to the Russian market. In the aftermath of the Soviet break-up, as Russia was passing through crisis and chaotic conditions, mafia elements in Russia badly affected market environment. There were unscrupulous businessmen in India too, who resorted to unfair methods that affected trade between the two countries. This situation seems to have changed now. Secondly, as opined by many analysts, there is an 'information gap' about the Russian market conditions contacts. During the Soviet era Indian companies were dealing with state sector organisations, which was safe and reliable. There has been a systemic change in the Russian economy and there might not be sufficient information about new Russian private sector companies, willing to trade with India as well as about the scope and prospects of Russian market for Indian goods. Thirdly, it is difficult for Indian firms to find out the credit worthiness of new Russian companies, and this itself makes dealings with such firms a risky proposition. What adds to the complexity of the situation is that quite often Russian banks do not provide credit reports of companies on behalf of which they conduct transactions. Hence this becomes a great bottleneck for some Indian firms to enter into transactions with a Russian counterpart. Fourthly, the ECGC coverage for exports to Russia is too expensive. This could be partly linked to the overall high risk factor that prevailed in the 1990s. However, it is worth noving that at present, with significant improvement in the Russian economy, ECGC has placed Russia in

Group 'A2' in the open cover category with normal percentage of cover. This may help overcome this constraint. Fifthly, respondents to a FICCI survey also pointed out that the insurance market in Russia is not adequately developed and there are hardly any products that provide insurance cover for stocks and raw materials. Sixthly, Indian businessmen feel the payment system involving letter of credit is ineffective in dealing with their counterparts in Russia. Seventhly, Indian exporters face a major problem of long duration of about two months and costly transportation of goods to be exported from India to Russia, since after the Soviet break-up goods are not sent through Odessa port which is in Ukraine. This constraint can be overcome if the proposed North-South corridor via Iran and the Caspian Sea can become a reality. But even as the proposal has been viable and feasible, which can reduce time and cost significantly, it has not become operative. Eighthly, many Indian businessmen who seem to be interested in promoting trade and economic ties with Russia face a major problem of cumbersome and time consuming 'visa-regime' of Russia. When political relations between the two countries have been consistently close and cordial, such a cumbersome visa regime goes against economic interest of both the countries. Lastly, some Indian business firms suffered losses in the 1990s when several Russian banks went but that severely affected trust in the Russian banking system. However, the banking problem has been largely overcome during the last few years with private sector Indian banks operating from Moscow or posting their representatives to operate on their behalf.

Russian companies do not face such problems in exporting to India. This is mainly because most of the Russian firms which export to India, for instance power equipments to Tehri hydro-power plant, machineries for construction sites, nuclear plant in Kudankulam etc deal with the government and public sector units as was the case during the Soviet era. Similarly, Russian organisations such as Gazprom and Tyuzpioexport provide equipment for modernisation of energy, metallurgical and chemical units in India which are in mainly in public sector. Hence Russia continues to deal with state sector units and do not face problem of 'information gap', lack of information about the customer and payment delays from Indian side. This has helped Russian companies to sustain and increase exports to India.

Initiatives and Policy Measures

There is no doubt that the policy-makers of both India and Russia have taken policy decisions and measures from time to time in order to promote trade and economic ties between the two countries. Moreover, there have been mutual exchanges of visits at all levels including at the apex political levels during which joint declarations are made and even trade targets are fixed. For instance, in 2006 the Indian Commerce Minister Kamal Nath and former Russian Economic and Trade Minister German Gref, during the latter's visit to India, set up of a Joint Study Group (JSG) with a view to examining the feasibility of signing a Comprehensive Economic Cooperation Agreement (CECA) between India and Russia, besides envisaging growth in bilateral trade turnover to US $ 10 billion by 2010. The JSG was expected to prepare by the end of 2006 a roadmap for achieving a significant increase in mutual trade turnover by diversifying and strengthening bilateral relations in a wide range of areas, particularly trade in goods and services, investment and economic cooperation. This was said to be another milestone in promoting India-Russia economic relations. Similarly, the former Russian president Vladimir Putin was the chief guest at the Republic Day parade in New Delhi in January 2007. This was a strong indication of underscoring importance India attaches to Russia. Equally important was the visit of the former Russian Prime Minister, Zubkov, to India in February 2008 following the visit of Manmohan Singh to Moscow in November 2007. All these high level visits are intended to strengthen political and economic ties between the two countries. For instance, the significance of the visit of Zubkov lies in the fact that it coincided with the second session-of-India-Russia Economic Forum on Trade and Investment, which was attended by over 500 business representatives of both the countries from both public and private sectors. India's leading trading organisations such as FICCI, CII, between the two countries and a Joint Task Force (JTF) which is expected to monitor the implementation of the recommendations of the Joint Study Group to push trade and economic ties to new heights by removing the impediments to bilateral trade and commerce. In the opinion of analysts there are good prospects of Indian and Russian companies working together in IT, financial services, power and energy sectors. Moreover, business groups of the two countries discussed cooperating in other key spheres such as transport, infrastructure, metallurgy and mining in both India and Russia. In this context it is worth noting that coinciding with Zubkov's visit to New Delhi, the Russian Vneshtorgbank (VTB) and Russian telecom and services conglomerate giant Sistema inaugurated their representative offices in New Delhi, which may help in enhancing trade and economic ties between the two countries. As stated by the Russian prime minister, India-Russia bilateral trade in 2007 was about $ 5 billion and between 2005 and 2007. This seems to include Russia's defence exports to India.

Futuristic Scenarios

Based on the above analyses of India-Russia economic relations, the following three futuristic scenarios can be visualised for the medium term of about three upcoming years - ambitious scenario, pessimistic scenario and pragmatic scenario. As mentioned above, in the ambitious, optimistic scenario, the policy-makers of both India and Russia have in their joint statements indicated that bilateral trade could reach a total of $ 10 billion by 2010. While setting such targets, it is pointed out that there is convergence of interests between the two countries and there is no doubt that huge potentialities exist for augmenting trade and strengthening economic ties. In visualising this scenario it is also expected that most of the problems affecting trade will be overcome in order to achieve the set goals. Hence some business organisations such as FICCI, while reiterating and supporting this view, opine that bilateral trade can cross $ 10 billion mark by 2010 and $ 20 billion level by 2015, adding a proviso "if trade irritants and procedural hassles are resolved". But some of the targets are rather ambitious and declarations seem to be political in nature and are an expression of pious intentions.

India's exports have shown downward trend over the years, and problems facing India-Russia trade have persisted. This implies that a 'pessimistic scenario' is not unlikely where India's export trade may stagnate at the present level. What adds to the credibility of this situation of many traditional agricultural products including tea from India.

The third pragmatic scenario predicts India-Russia mutual trade turnover to reach about $7-8 billion by 2010. Although an upswing is evident in the last few years in India's exports to and imports from Russia, several problems in trade relations persist. It is unlikely that all the problems facing Indian export firms are resolved overnight. Hence while India's imports from Russia may continue to rise significantly, there could be only modest increase in India's exports to Russia. With joint state level efforts and cooperation between India and Russia, and if some of the major constraints in trade are overcome, then Indian businessmen might be able to maintain the level of exports of traditional items and also register increase in non-traditional items including pharmaceuticals and engineering products to Russia. It is hoped that efforts in the direction of joint ventures in Russia for manufacturing also could yield results.

Table 1: India-Russia Imports and Exports Trade

(Million US dollars)

	1991-92	*2000-01*	*2003-04*	*2004-05*	*2006-7*
(a) India's Exports to Russia	1,640	869.9	714.2	631.0	907.6
(b) India's Imports From Russia	728	517.2	960.3	1322.2	1940.9
(c) Total Trade Turnover	2368	1.387.1	1674.5	-6912	2847.5 (Ex+IM)
(d) Trade Balance	912	352.7	-146.1	-3293	-10333 (Ex-Im)

Table 2: India's Exports to Russia of Major Commodities

(Million US dollars)

Year	*Tea*	*Pharma*	*RMG of cotton*	*Coffee*	*Cotton Yam Fab*
2000	105	109	208	63	57
2007	61	271	56	51	
Net change	-43	+162	-132	-12	-34

18

India-Russia Bilateral Relations are Intensifying but Challenges Persist

The Indian Prime Minister Narendra Modi had the latest meeting with the Russian president Vladimir Putin at G-20 summit in China in September 2016 even as both the leaders have met several times during the last about two years reconfirming the chemistry of close and cordial bilateral relations and Russia consistently supporting India in various regional and global organisations. For instance, both the leaders met in Tashkent on 26th June 2016 on the sidelines of SCO meeting during which Putin welcomed India signing the Memorandum of Obligations of SCO that has kick-started the process of India's accession as 'full member' into this powerful regional grouping since India will have to sign around 30 other documents to complete the process for membership. In addition to that in 2016 India has assumed chairmanship of the BRICS and its Bank which is an influential bloc comprising five countries Brazil-China-India-Russia and South Africa. The importance of BRICS lies in the fact that it constitutes 42 percent of the world population and combined GDP of over US$ 16 trillion. Equally important is the fact that India will host the BRICS summit in 2016. An effort has been made in this paper to analyze efforts being made by both India and Russia to intensify multidimensional bilateral ties as also the challenges in achieving the objectives.

Nuclear Energy

India is rightly putting in place a long-term strategy of transition from dependence on oil to non-fossil fuels including nuclear energy as highlighted by leading energy expert and president of the World Energy Policy Summit Narendra Taneja. Kudankulam Nuclear Plant (KNPP) is the primer and largest Russian-India project in the energy sector conceived in 1988 during the Soviet era has been expanding being an important component of the strategic partnership between Russia and India. The significance of KNPP lies in the following- Firstly, the KNPP located in Tamil Nadu provides power not only to the state of Tamil Nadu but also partly to the states of Kerala, Karnataka, Andhra Pradesh and Union Territory of Puducherry. Russia's Rosatom and the Nuclear Power Corporation of India Limited (NPCIL) took initiative to revive and expedite the delayed project which was launched in 2012. Commercial operation of the second unit of India's KNPP is expected to start in December 2016 when the total capacity of nuclear power generation in India will grow to nearly 7,000 megawatts. Some analysts opine that these two projects will provide a reliable supply source of electricity required for India's growing industrial development.

Secondly, KNPP has played a pioneering role by working out specific plans with Russia to build up to 25 nuclear power plants in India in the next few years. Hence Russian official Andrievsky has stated that both the countries intend to have long-term and fruitful cooperation. Equally important is the fact that KNPP has played an important role in promoting Russia's image in global energy sector and "global expansion of Rosatom", which has set up nuclear plants in China and Iran.

Thirdly, it is a matter of great significance for India that in June 2016 Russia bestowed a top honor "order of friendship" on Dr. R. S. Sundar, the director of KNPP acknowledging his immense contribution in India-Russia nuclear energy field.

Fourthly, Russia is not only the first country to supply nuclear fuel and technology, but will also be the first country for drafting a roadmap for supporting production of components for nuclear fuel reactors of Russian design in the next ten years as stated by the

Vice-President of the Tvel - fuel company of Rosatom Oleg Grigoriev in August 2016. This will further enhance India's status globally in nuclear energy field.

Fifthly, while Russia has been the pioneer in promoting nuclear energy in India, there is competition from other giants. For instance, Toshiba Corp's Westinghouse Electric, Japanese-owned US company and GE-Hitachi, announced that they will be relocating a proposed project to build six nuclear reactors. However, outbidding other players, in July 2016 there was a delegation to Russia led by Indian Commerce Minister Nirmala Sitharaman along with Chandrababu Naidu during which as reported by Sputnik, Rosatom is likely to build six power plants in the state of Andhra Pradesh. 1,200 MW VVER Nuclear Reactors will be constructed there with the safest, most up-to-date technology. If everything goes according to plan, Andhra Pradesh will be home to more than a dozen nuclear reactors.

Lastly, while India aims to create 15,000 megatons of uranium reserve to fuel its nuclear reactors, as reported by the government sources, Russia is the biggest contributor to India's 'strategic uranium reserve' apart from Kazakhstan and Canada to supply uranium to India.

Defence Sector

India and Russia share a "special and privileged strategic relationship" that has helped India to make significant scientific and technological progress in defence sector. Mention may be made of the fact that BrahMos missiles are already operational that has strengthened India's defence capability with due support from Russia. India has worked out plans in 2016 to arm three regiments of Su-30MKI fighter jets with BrahMos missiles. Moreover, as opined by some defence analysts, India and Russia can co-produce and sell the supersonic 'BrahMos' missile, which has a range of 290 kilometres, to third countries.

Secondly, as stated by a Russian defence expert, India is interested to purchase an additional 40 multifunctional Su-30MKI fighters, in addition to the 210 such machines that were already in service. The aircrafts are assembled from the Russian kits at the Indian HAL Corporation and will cost India $ 3 billion which is a very competitive price. Moreover, as per Russia reports on 11th July 2016 India was finally taking forward the negotiations with Russia on stalled projects to jointly develop a futuristic fifth-generation fighter aircrafts as well as upgrade its existing Su-30MKI jets to 'Super Sukhois' with advanced avionics and weapons. This is a positive development since as stated by India's defence minister Manohar Parrikar, serviceability of Russia's Sukhois has jumped to 60 percent from 46 percent earlier since Indian defence sector facing shortage of fighter squadron and cannot depend upon obsolete MiG-21 and MiG-27. Moreover, in March 2016 the Indian Air Force conducted acceptance testing of the first two auxiliary power units (APU), renovated by the Russian holding company "Technodinamika" for the military transport aircraft IL-76, and its modifications.

Thirdly, supporting India's policy of "Make in India", Russian representative of Rosoboronexport, Mr. Goreslavsky has opined that strategic projects will function on the basis of intergovernmental agreements with due participation of private sector in joint ventures. He mentioned the pilot project that involves production of Russian Ka-226 helicopters in India will be the first to meet the requirements under this principle. However, he added that Russia faces competition in India's growing defence market. In August 2016 Russia's Deputy Industry and Trade Minister Aleksandr Potapov stressed importance of Russia-India cooperation in aviation sector including proposal to sell Russia's Sukhoi Superjet-100 airliner. He also mentioned about production of India's own regional plane that may become an important joint project in civil aircraft building along with HAL to produce Ilyushin-114-300. If that materialises according to Russian experts, by 2020 India will emerge to the position of the world's third largest aircraft market. Thus, Russia has keen interest in promoting ambitious joint ventures with India making it a major partner in the Asian region in defence sector which has been reconfirmed by Russia at the 20th anniversary of the Russia-ASEAN partnership meeting held in Singapore in June 2016.

Fourthly, it is a matter of great significance that in June 2016 India became the 35th country to be admitted to the Missile Technology Control Regime (MTCR), a major international anti-proliferation group of which Russia is a key member. This should enable easier space and missile collaboration for India with Russia, which could not supply cryogenic engines and other dual use technology missiles to India, because it was bound by MTCR norms. Moreover, Russia backs India's bid to become a Nuclear Supplier Group (NSG) member, and has even stated that it was ready to assist in arriving at a "positive decision" for India to join the elite nuclear commerce club. In this context India has confirmed in June 2016 that it had launched a high-power campaign aimed at "engaging all members of the Nuclear Suppliers Group" in Geneva to seek support for India. The NSG plenary meeting was held in Seoul, Republic of Korea, on 23rd and 24th May 2016 during which India's application to enter the NSG was a part of discussion. In this regard in June 2016 India's Foreign minister Mrs Sushma Swaraj spoke personally to the Russian foreign Minister Sergey Lavrov who conveyed Russia's support to India to become a member. While seeking support from China has been a difficult task, she has expressed her hope that India could become a member of the NSG by the end of 2016. In fact, India's Foreign Secretary Subrahmanyam Jaishankar, also visited Beijing on 16th and 17th June 2016 for bilateral talks during which all issues including NSG membership.

Fifthly, during the last few years India has taken a right policy of diversifying the sources for defence supplies and as a result USA and France have also become important suppliers of defence equipments. France has developed close ties with India and has finalised deal estimated at €7.8 billion for supplying 36 Rafael jets and started supplying jets in September 2016 strengthening India's defence capability. With these developments Russia's share in India's defence imports has declined to about 55-60 percent as against over 80 percent in the past. While acknowledging that the relationship in the area of defence ties with the United States has been growing strong, Mrs. Sushma Swaraj was candid in stating that they were not at the cost of "our friend Russia."

Energy Sector

India has been a major importer of oil and natural gas being deficient in hydrocarbon resources. During the Soviet era, USSR endowed with huge hydrocarbon resources was a major exporter of oil to India but there has been a substantial decline in post-Soviet Russia's share in India's import. However, during the last over a decade India and Russia have evolved bilateral ties in the energy sector in different ways to promote their common interest.

Firstly, a new development in this bilateral relation is that oil companies in both the countries are engaged in not only trading oil and gas but buying and selling stakes. For instance, in August 2016 according to Russian news agency Sputnik, Indian state-owned Oil and Natural Gas Corporation ONGC Videsh Ltd. (OVL), which has been actively operating in Russia's energy sector, is exploring the opportunity to acquire a 49 percent stake in Russian oil producer Rosneft Oil Co.'s Tagul field. In a similar case the Government of India seems to have approved the acquisition by the Indian Oil and Gas Corporation a 15 percent stake in Vankor Field from Rosneft. At the same time there is reciprocity from Russian side since as per Indian media reports in May 2016, Rosneft has proposed to buy 74 percent of Indian Essar Oil company which has decreased its debt by more than $ 6.7 billion. Both Rosneft and Indian Essar Oil Company and both are partners in refinery located in Vadinar.

Secondly, an equally interesting case is Russia's arctic region which is rich in hydrocarbon resources. In this context Sergey Donskoy, head of Russia's Ministry of Natural Resources stated that Rosneft was in negotiations with ONGC to jointly participate in offshore projects in the Arctic region. It is claimed that there is positive response as India has announced its readiness to participate financially in the exploration and development of Arctic oil and gas deposits, which has some risk.

Thirdly, it is matter of importance that being hit by economic sanctions by the West due to alleged annexation of Crimea, Russia has been interested in seeking foreign investment in energy sector which is a major exporter of oil and gas. This is confirmed by the statement by ambassador Gleb Ivashentsov, member of the Russian International Affairs Council in July 2016 that facing financial crunch due to sanctions by the West, Russia is interested in attracting funds from China and India and in return Russia will export liquefied natural gas at competitive prices. Hence there will be reciprocity in such deals which benefit all the partners.

Fourthly, as Indian companies create their own resource base in Russia, the question will arise as to the best method of delivery of energy resources to the Indian subcontinent. While a pipeline may be the most convenient and cheapest way to supply liquefied natural gas from Russia to India by pipeline, this is over ambitious involving $ 30 billion investment. Alternatively transporting through tankers is realistic. Thus, a few strategies for transporting oil and natural gas to India are being studied, including the route through the Chinese Xinjiang Uygur Autonomous Region and swapping gas supplies to Iran.

Fifthly, the proposal of North-South corridor linking the Caspian Sea via Iran with Indian Ocean which can facilitate transport of oil and natural gas to India has been unduly delayed. Similarly, subsequent to the visit of the Indian prime minister to Central Asia in 2016, proposal of TAPI pipeline hit headlines under which India would be able to get oil from Turkmenistan via Afghanistan and Pakistan. Even as some analysts were supportive of this project, it is highly unlikely under adverse prevailing adverse political conditions in the region.

Terrorism

Both India and Russia have become victims of terrorism during the last few years which has also become a global problem. The Indian foreign minister Mrs Swaraj highlighted the problem of terrorism emanating from Pakistan at the UN 1267 Committee (on terrorism) and also at the Russia, India and China (RIC) ministerial meeting in Moscow. It is unfortunate that China has not been supportive and had blocked the designation of Masood Azhar as an international terrorist, whom India contended that he was responsible for a terrorist attack in Pathankot air base in January 2016. Subsequently the Indian prime minister has asserted this global problem during the G-20 meeting in China in September 2016. Similarly, the role of Pakistan for terrorist violence in Kashmir is being taken up by India's home minister Mr. Rajnath Singh who made special visits to Moscow and Washington in September 2016.

Economic Cooperation

Trade and economic ties continue to be weak link in India-Russia bilateral relations. Hence Putin was frank in stating in June 2016 that trade turnover between India and Russia is too small and does not correspond to the potential. This was also reiterated by Yaroslav Tarasyuk, the Russian Trade Representative in India that during the last three years India-Russia trade turnover has been falling which is about $ 7-8 billion. According to 2014 Russian data, for Russia, India was in 19th place in terms of turnover, while for India, Russia was in 34th place. In 2015 this turnover further reduced by another 20 percent. This unsatisfactory performance is in sharp contrast to the past when Soviet Union was the leading trading partner accounting for about 12-14 percent of India's total trade turnover. Hence there has been a stark realisation on the part of leaders of India and Russia that given close and cordial political ties not only efforts are needed to increase bilateral trade, but also deeper cooperation at the institutional level, between the relevant ministries and institutions. It is appreciable that to realise potentialities, some major policy decisions and measures have been undertaken to strengthen economic ties during the last couple of years.

Firstly, the bilateral meeting of India's External Affairs Minister Ms. Sushma Swaraj with her Russian counterpart, Deputy Prime Minister Dmitry Rogozin on 22nd October 2015 reinforced India's "special and privileged strategic partnership" with the intention to implement the "Druzhba-Dosti" vision of President Vladimir Putin and Prime Minister Narendra Modi, through concrete initiatives in different fields of bilateral trade and economic cooperation over the next decade. In fact, this reiterates prime minister's slogan at his inaugural address that India is blessed with three "D"s: Democracy, Demography and Demand". He added a fourth "D" that is Deregulation in order to achieve India's ambitions to become the investment hub of the world. This should be an indicator for Russia which has an ambitious plan to achieve the bilateral annual trade turnover with India of $30 billion and $ 15 billion of mutual investment by 2025. The Russian minister assured that on its part Russia was taking "steps to create favourable conditions for developing trade, economic and investment cooperation, particularly free trade agreement, agreement on mutual stimulation and protection of investment, on payments in national currencies, on admitting certifications of conformity and education and diploma standards."

Secondly, St. Petersburg International Economic Forum (SPIEF) held in Russia in June 2016 was attended by ten thousand participants from 70 countries was an important event promoting Russia's foreign trade and economic ties. The Russian president Mr. Vladimir Putin specifically mentioned at the inauguration of SPIEF, the scope for India in enhancing economic ties with the Eurasian Economic Union (EEU) initiated by Russia which has enormous market potential. As a part of this Forum, business conference round table "Russia - India: new stage of economic partnership" was held in which India was represented by Ramesh Abhishek, Deputy Minister of Trade and Industry, Darius Naushad Forbes, president of the Confederation of Indian Industry and Pankaj Saran, Indian Ambassador to Russia, among others. Russian side was represented by Alexei Likhachev, First Deputy Minister of Economic Development who outlined the projected thrust areas to boost bilateral economic cooperation and that Russia has developed a number of mechanisms such as a special investment contract, special economic zones, exchange of services and preferential conditions for investors in each region. Thus, as the private sector that is going to fuel the economies of Russia and India in the long run and if SMEs get the right amount of support and encouragement, they could be the force that powers Indo-Russian trade to new levels particularly for startup companies which have the potential to be major employment generators in both countries and could also fuel a technology boom. Hence to pursue these policy initiatives, India and Russia have set up Working Group on Modernisation and Industrial Cooperation and in the fifth meeting of this organisation several fields have been identified for joint ventures in the field of mineral, fertilizers, power equipment, CRGO steel, pharmaceutical etc.

Thirdly, at the INNOPROM (Industrial Innovation) held in July 2016 in Russia's city of Ekaterensburg, several MoUs have been signed between Russian and Indian enterprises, with the former expressing an enthusiasm to be a part of Narendra Modi's 'Make in India' initiative. While such response is appreciable, implementation of this policy will be a test case for both the countries. At the opening session, Russian Industry and Trade Minister Denis Manturov emphasised that Russia was setting priority for the development of cutting-edge inventions in industrial sectors, including industrial Internet, robotics and areas, such as technologies for processing industrial waste, biotechnology and alternative energy. Russia has potentiality which needs to be promoted by state and non-state actors. In this context Yaroslav Tarasyuk, the Russian Trade Representative in India has been candid in stating that in Russia, there are many companies with interesting developments, but they lack resources to commercialise them. Hence Indian companies can help commercialize these developments, with an eye on not only the Indian market, but also for potential sale to third countries, like West Asia, with whom they have good contacts. As opined by Russian analyst Natalya Rudkova, INNOPROM has potentiality to usher in a new era of bilateral economic activity, for reviving and bolstering Russian and Indian cooperation, trade and prosperity. This is evident from the fact that the Russian Prime Minister Medvedev visited three stalls of Indian Pavilion which was attended by Ms Nirmala Sitharaman India's Minister of State for Commerce and Industry and the three Chief Ministers of India, namely, Maharashtra, Rajasthan and Andhra Pradesh apart from representatives of 110 companies and senior government officials. Sitharaman informed Medvedev that the BRICS Industries Ministers' meeting would be held before the forthcoming BRICS Summit in Goa in October 2016.

Hence there are expectations of bilateral economic ties might expand considering the fact that following agreements have been signed, (a) between the Development Corporation of the Moscow region and Indian the Confederation of Indian Industry, (b) SRB International which is one of the largest Indian suppliers of equipment, and implements turnkey projects in mining, metallurgy, and the oil and gas industry signed cooperation agreements with three Russian companies including well known Uralkhimmash, engaged in machine building and chemical engineering. Uralmash and SRB International have cooperated in supplying and servicing heavy equipment to several Indian companies during the last many years. Russian analyst opine that besides Uralmash, many Russian companies have already shown interest to invest in the manufacturing and mining sectors in India which might support implementing India's "Make in India" and "Skill India" policy of the Indian government to produce high quality products, (c) Uralvagonzavod signed agreement with the Kalyani Group to promote UVZ products in India, (d) Sukhoi Civil Aircraft Company has proposed to sign an agreement with Indian company Tata Advanced Systems (part of the Tata Group), for the manufacture of spare parts for the passenger aircraft Sukhoi Superjet 100 (SSJ-100).

Fourthly, it is appreciable that some Russian companies have succeeded in joint ventures in India. For instance, in 2016 a joint venture between Mosmetrostroy (founded in 1931) and Hindustan Construction Company Ltd (HCC) bagged a $372 million (Rs 2,523 crore) contract to construct part of the underground metro line in Mumbai. Santosh Rai, Head, Transport Sales of HCC is confident of experience and expertise of both organisations for successful completion of project.

Fifthly, the role and contribution of some chief ministers of India needs to be appreciated. For instance, Mrs. Vasundhara Raje Scindia, Chief Minister of Rajasthan has stated that industry ministers of Rajasthan and Sverdlovsk regions have been tasked to prepare a detailed plan on cooperation in the timber industry and heavy engineering. Moreover, Raje invited businessmen from Sverdlovsk to an agricultural exhibition, due to be held in India in November 2016, and to the global investors summit in Rajasthan in 2017.

Sixthly, reinforcing scope for enhancing economic ties Gopal V Rajagopalan, General Secretary, IBA, has opined that the Russian market has stabilised after its initial upheaval following the currency devaluation. In fact the downward trend of the Russian Rouble has facilitated exports from Russia to other markets, including India, with demand for paper, timber and chemicals from Russia. This seems to be evident from the fact in May 2016 Alexander Potapov, executive director and member of the Board of Directors at the Russian Venture Company OJSC, outlined his company's plans to raise bilateral trade ties with India and that RVC has decided to open a representative office in India so that Russia will have opportunities for its technology companies to manufacture their products and provide services using Indian production chains.

Seventhly, India has been an important country exporting traditional goods to Russia including tea, tobacco, spices etc. whose share has declined after the Soviet breakup in total export basket. Considering the fact that as Russia has been subjected to embargo from Europe on the issue of Ukraine, there is opportunity for India to increase export traditional goods as also buffalo meat, dairy products and cheese to Russia.

Eighthly, during the last couple of years, Asian countries have gained prominence accounting for 90 percent in Russia's foreign investment sector in 2015 partly due to economic sanctions by Europe. In this context as opined Russian economic analysts, apart from China, India, South Korea and the Gulf states, the BRICS New Development Bank and the Asian Infrastructure Investment Bank play a critical role. It is widely known that among G-20 India has been a fast growing economy apart from China. Hence Russia's 'Look East' policy is understandable and evident in promoting external economic ties. Similarly, Eurasian Economic Union in which Russia, Kazakhstan, Belorussia, Armenia and Kyrgyzstan are members has also emerged as an important organisation and a huge market is looking for enhancing economic ties with India. Moreover, the Commercial Indo Bank (a joint venture of State Bank of India and Canara Bank) had started operations in Russia. In view of this there is immense scope for increasing trade in the field of IT, pharmaceutical, tourism and medical tourism.

Ninthly, one of the main items that India exports to Russia is pharmaceutical products. Many discussions are now taking place about companies that sell their drugs in the Russian market could move their production facilities to Russia. For example, one of the largest Indian pharmaceutical companies, Lupin, has now confirmed that it has purchased the Russian pharmaceutical manufacturer Biocom in the Stavropol Krai, to manufacture its products at an already operating plant. In this regard there is immense scope for Indian and Russian pharma companies such as Glenmark, Dr Reddy Labs to increase exports and also to jointly set up plants in Russia to produce a wide range of medicines to meet growing demand in Russia and EEU countries for high quality drugs of high international standard and at low price as compared to those from the West.

Constraints and Challenges

Notwithstanding certain achievements in promoting bilateral ties, there are constraints and challenges in boosting economic ties. Firstly, one of the major constraint affecting trade is that it takes a long time and involves high cost for transportation of goods from India to Russia due to lack of availability of Black Sea port facilities that prevailed in the past. Crimea on the Black Sea was the hub of trading activities has now been regained by Russia that can play major role in enhancing and promoting international trade and defence ties. As opined by Admiral Vladimir Komoedov, chairman of the State Duma Committee for Defence in July 2016, the construction of the Crimean Bridge linking Crimea with Russia can become a stimulus to develop Russian-Indian logistics and port projects in the Crimea. Even as it is highly speculative at present due to Russia's conflict with Ukraine on this issue, it may become a reality in the near future linking Mumbai port with the port in Sevastopol.

Secondly, as an alternative route, India has been hoping and eagerly waiting materialisation of North-South corridor via Iran, Caspian Sea to Astrakhan that will reduce the time of transportation of goods from the present 40 days to 15-20 days. In fact, North-South Corridor will boost India's economic ties not only with Russia but also with many countries of the Common Wealth of Independent states such as Azerbaijan, Turkmenistan and Kazakhstan which were part of former Soviet Union and with which India has close and cordial relations. There are high hopes with regard to this delayed project since as reported by Russian media analyst Igor Zubkov on 16th May 2016, Russian authorities are expecting that the North-South International Transport Corridor (ITC), which is indeed a complicated logistics, will start operating soon, which would involve cargo shipments through Iran. This will be highly economical since the cost of transporting a 40-foot container from Mumbai (India) to Moscow, through Iran and Azerbaijan, will not exceed $3,000.

Thirdly, a Russian analyst has contended that in India, Russian-made machinery and equipment are taxed at rates from 10-30 percent, and this presents a serious constraint for Russian exporters. If customs fees are substantially reduced, then the opportunities for these manufacturers will be much wider. Perhaps this might be possible when India and Russia sign free trade agreement as India has signed a free trade zone agreement with the Republic of Korea.

Fourthly, according to some critics it is still not very easy for small-scale Indian businessmen to get a Russian visa and there is information gap about trading opportunities. On this issue Russia contends that such negative information is wrong created by the West. At the same time efforts are being made by the Russian government agencies to open information centers, organising exhibitions to help trading partners to support economic relations with Russia. Rules regarding work permits should be simplified by both countries.

Fifthly, some western analysts opine that investment climate in Russia has been poor due to bureaucratic hurdles and restrictive policies of reducing the share of foreign investment in oil and natural gas. But denying such views it is contended that Russia's position in the Doing Business World Bank Rankings has been improving (In 2015 Russia jumped 11 steps from 62nd to 51st place in 2016 out of 183 countries). In support of this Ramnik Singh Kohli, head of Micromax in Russia, has been candid in stating that his company had not experienced any bureaucratic delays and enjoyed a seven percent market share in their segment of mobile instruments. However, he stressed the need for a B2B platform for promoting trade ties and better banking system for facilitating bilateral trade. In this regard Vladimir Goshin, Minister in charge of Customs Cooperation has stated that single window custom clearance system which is currently being developed should be a breakthrough in Eurasian Economic cooperation, bringing down paperwork and costs. However, it needs to be noted that Russian economy has been facing economic crisis condition that is affecting external trade and even retail trade declined by ten percent in 2015. Similarly, the concept of Russia to shift bilateral trade in national currencies, is rather difficult and complicated since banking systems are not ready for being involved in the process.

Sixthly, there is a view among Indian exporters to Russia that unlike the former Soviet Union many Russian trading firms give preference to import from Western countries as against import from India due to quality, delivery schedule etc. But this issue has been contested by Gopal V Rajagopalan, General Secretary, IBA stating that Indian businessmen were also responsible for their poor image in the Russian market because they strictly adhere to deadlines and quality control while exporting to the West and not to the Russian market.

Thus, in conclusion it may be stated that several policy decisions are taken by India and Russia to intensify bilateral political and strategic ties. Measures to reform and liberalise the economy are declared by Russia for enhancing trade and investment even as challenges persist in their implementation.

Index

F

G

N

S

X

Y